# TRUE COLORS
## STORIES OF BAPTIST INCLUSION

Foreword by Bill J. Leonard
Jake Hall, Editor

© 2023
Published in the United States by Nurturing Faith, Macon, GA.
Nurturing Faith is a book imprint of Good Faith Media (goodfaithmedia.org).
Library of Congress Cataloging-in-Publication Data is available.

ISBN: 978-1-63528-222-1

All rights reserved. Printed in the United States of America.

Scripture quotations marked NRSV are from the Revised Standard Version of the Bible, copyright © 1946, 1952, and 1971 National Council of the Churches of Christ in the United States of America. Used by permission. All rights reserved worldwide.

Scripture quotations marked (NIV) are taken from the Holy Bible, New International Version®, NIV®. Copyright © 1973, 1978, 1984, 2011 by Biblica, Inc.™ Used by permission of Zondervan. All rights reserved worldwide. www.zondervan.com The "NIV" and "New International Version" are trademarks registered in the United States Patent and Trademark Office by Biblica, Inc.™

Cover color image by Gerd Altmann from Pixabay.

# Acknowledgments

We are deeply grateful to the many individuals and organizations who have supported and contributed to this book project.

We would like to begin by expressing our gratitude to Good Faith Media, whose commitment to telling the untold stories has made this book possible. Your dedication to publishing books that challenge and inspire is truly admirable.

We are also grateful to the Eula Mae and John Baugh Foundation, whose generous grant has enabled us to produce this book. Your support for progressive, inclusive, nonprofit organizations that reflect the love of Christ is inspiring. Your passion for keeping faith communities informed and engaged has had a significant impact on our communities.

We would like to acknowledge the editorial team who helped to shape this book and bring it to fruition. Thank you to Rev. Dr. Erin Hall of Renford Collective and to Jean Trotter and Kelley Land of Faithlab for your dedication to this project and your insights and contributions to the final product.

This book is dedicated to all those who have worked and continue to work toward a more inclusive and compassionate church. May it inspire us to see the world in all its vibrant and diverse colors and to move into a future where all are welcomed and affirmed.

# Contents

Preface ........................................................................................................ 1

Foreword by *Bill J. Leonard* ...................................................................... 3

Chapter 1: The Perils of Purple Churches ............................................... 9
    *Jake Hall*

Chapter 2: On Reading Scripture—and Our Neighbors—Well ........... 17
    *Preston Clegg*

Chapter 3: Catharsis in Communion ..................................................... 25
    *Jay Hogewood*

Chapter 4: Holy Moments and Hallowed Ground ................................ 33
    *Carol McEntyre*

Chapter 5: A Matter of Life and Death .................................................. 41
    *George A. Mason*

Chapter 6: Examine the Fruits ................................................................ 49
    *Jeremy Hall*

Chapter 7: Fully Alive .............................................................................. 57
    *Rich Havard*

Chapter 8: Travelers on a Journey ........................................................... 63
    *Scott Dickison*

Chapter 9: The Blind Leading the Blind ................................................ 73
    *Erica Whitaker*

Chapter 10: Your Story, Our Story, God's Story .................................... 81
    *Cody J. Sanders*

Chapter 11: You Are Welcome, But… .................................................... 89
    *Timothy Peoples*

Chapter 12: At Last, Your Truth ............................................................. 95
    *Junia Joplin*

Chapter 13: How Homophobia Leads to Universalism ....................... 103
    *Brett Younger*

Chapter 14: Betting It All On Love ...................................................... 113
    *Elizabeth Mangham Lott*

# Preface

The beauty of a prism lies in the way it refracts light, revealing the colors that are hidden within it. Each facet of the prism offers a new perspective, a new way of seeing the world around us.

In much the same way, the contributors to this volume offer a range of experiences around LGBTQ+ inclusion in the Baptist tradition. They are like the facets of a prism, each reflecting a different aspect of the light that shines on this complex and contentious issue.

Each contributor has served as a congregational minister, and each has come to understand the love of God in Christ in a different way, both within themselves and within their congregations and contexts. Through their essays, they reveal the true colors of inclusion—colors that have too often been dimmed or dismissed within the church. They expose alternative readings of the text, theological frameworks, and leadership strategies that shade and diminish the fullness of the body of Christ.

These honest readings of the Bible and fresh theological frameworks provide insights into the lived experience of LGBTQ+ persons and their congregations. The essays are not only thoughtful and engaging but also deeply personal and transformative. Each contributor shares their own journey of understanding and their own struggle to fully embody the good news and to lead their congregations to do the same. They invite deeper conversation on the expansive love of God in Christ.

In a world that often seems divided and polarized, the contributors to *True Colors: Stories of Baptist Inclusion* offer a vision of the church as a place of welcome and beauty. They challenge us to see beyond the narrow confines of tradition and orthodoxy and to embrace the full spectrum of human experience and diversity.

We hope that this volume will be a valuable resource for pastors, congregations, and individuals seeking to deepen their understanding and live out the call to love and justice that is at the heart of the gospel. May it inspire us to see the world in all its vibrant and diverse colors and to work together to build a more inclusive and compassionate church.

Rev. Dr. Jake Hall

# Foreword

## Dr. Bill J. Leonard

*Dr. Bill J. Leonard is a Founding Dean, Professor Emeritus at Wake Forest University School of Divinity, and author of 26 books.*

Reading the essays in this volume reminded me of a passage from Frederick Buechner's 1982 autobiographical text, *The Sacred Journey*. The late Presbyterian preacher/writer comments, "One way or another the journey through time starts for us all, and for all of us too, that journey is in at least one sense the same journey because what it is primarily, I think, is a journey in search." Buechner suggests that each of us must determine the nature of that search, noting that while "there will be as many answers as there are searchers," there also are "certain general answers" that include three common quests. Buechner says, "We search for a self to be. We search for other selves to love. We search for work to do."[1]

The contributors to *True Colors* testify to the nature of their searches, informed by issues of sexuality and spirituality. The contributors who write from inside the LGBTQ+ community reflect on their "search for a self to be," detailing many of the struggles they confronted in coming to terms with their sexual orientation or gender identity. They describe a sense of self they believe to be inherent in their identity as human beings. It was no easy exploration, but it was one that carried them through issues of guilt, secrecy, fear, alienation, and in some cases exile, often highlighted by their decision to "come out" to friends, family, and the world in which they live.

In another 1982 study, *Embracing the Exile*, therapist John E. Fortunato, who identifies himself as both "gay and Christian," wrote,

> Disownment or rejection by family—often the norm for gay people—is different from family turmoil revolving around an adolescent's adjustment at puberty, or a daughter who, at twenty-two, is trying to cut the umbilical cord, or a son who is about to marry a woman his parents don't like. It's different because, unlike these other situations, it's not how a son or daughter is *acting* that's being rejected, it's who they *are* constitutionally. They don't have a choice about being gay, there isn't anything inherently destructive in their sexual orientation, and yet, once found

out, they are treated like lepers by the people who supposedly love them the most.[2]

Writing four decades ago, Fortunato sought to offer hope to people in what is now referred to as the LGBTQ+ community. Implicitly and explicitly, he longed for social changes that became twenty-first-century realities including legalizing same-sex marriage, the development of "welcoming and affirming" congregations in multiple Christian denominations, and an increasing acceptance of LGBTQ+ persons and relationships in public and private life.

In 2022, Gallup's annual Mood of the Nation survey suggested that "while satisfaction on many of the other issues decreased this year, the numbers on gay and lesbian individuals grew substantially: In 2022, 62% of survey respondents said they were very or somewhat satisfied with the acceptance of gays and lesbians in the nation, up from 55% in 2021 and 56% in 2020."[3] At the same time, there is increasing evidence of significant legislative and ecclesiastical backlash against such progress, evidenced in new laws aimed at people who are transgender, "Don't Say Gay" regulations in public education, and increasing violence toward LGBTQ+ persons and communities. Ecclesiastically, a number of Christian congregations now require members to sign anti-LGBTQ+ doctrinal statements or be dismissed from the church rolls.[4] The LGBTQ+ contributors in this book acknowledge those stark realities, while insisting that they were compelled to pursue searches for their true self.

The contributors who detail their congregational journeys of response to LGBTQ+ people indicate that those faith communities were also involved in a "search for a self to be." They acknowledge the sometimes hesitant journeys of congregations toward recognizing, and ultimately affirming, the authentic self at the heart of those who have come to terms with their sexual orientation. Some acknowledge that the decision of certain churches to be "welcoming and affirming" to, for, and with LGBTQ+ individuals involved decisions about congregational "selfhood" and the nature of the gospel itself, discoveries not without churchly division and denominational dismissal.

The LGBTQ+ folks whose essays appear here confirm that a sense of self shaped the search "for other selves to love" amid cultural, familial, political, and ecclesiastical resistance. The ministers and congregations described here confess that their concern to live out the "Jesus Way" led them to expand their search "for other selves to love" by reaching out to people in the LGBTQ+ community and others on the cultural and churchly margins. That decision impacted—indeed, expanded—their own sense of self and gospel. In her *True Colors* essay, Baptist minister Elizabeth Mangham Lott notes,

To preach Jesus week in and week out required me to consider how wide and long and high and deep the love of God might be. I shared sermons about a man crossing the boundaries of Galilee and Samaria without regard to purity codes, eating with crooked tax collectors and rumored sex workers, restoring those cast out of community because of physical or mental illness, and reserving his harshest critiques for religious insiders who thought they were preserving the right things by keeping "those people" out.

In his 2013 study, *Queer Lessons for Churches on the Straight and Narrow*, Cody Sanders, pastor, professor, and contributor to this book, asks how loving relationships exemplified in same-sex marriages might reshape churchly responses to marriage itself. He writes,

> If we could appreciate the possibilities opened to us by the shifting nature of social, legal, and religious conceptions of marriage, rather than fear these changes, might we discover some potential for growth? If churches possessed a bit of wonderment, rather than dread, over the abilities of queer people to forge intimate partnerships and covenanted relationships despite decades and decades of nearly total opposition from every corner of society, we might find ourselves asking: *"What have queer people learned about the formation of relationships that we would all benefit from knowing?"*[5]

In that brief passage, Sanders challenges both gay and straight Christians to pursue Buechner's idea that "we search for work to do" as something that the two communities can do in exploring the work of the gospel together. In his *True Colors* chapter, Sanders is equally direct, urging progressive congregations to consider LGBTQ+ people in their midst as full co-laborers in the work of the gospel. He writes,

> as bearers of the Good News—and the belovedness and belonging of LGBTQ+ people is especially "good news"—we've got to be storytellers of that goodness. We learned that lesson from Jesus! And if the only place we endeavor to tell the Good News story is inside the walls of our churches, there are many who will never experience it.

Sanders and Elizabeth Mangham Lott, like other writers in this book, remind us that the search for a self to be, others to love, and work to do sends us to scripture and the Jesus Story. In Luke 4, Jesus references the prophet Isaiah in describing the work he was to do and, by implication, the work of those who follow him. It is a calling

> …to bring good news to the poor.
> To proclaim release to the captives
> and recovery of sight to the blind,
> to set free those who are oppressed,
> to proclaim the year of the Lord's favor. (4:18-19)

Reading that text in his hometown synagogue, Jesus expands it to include an array of outsiders, noting that "in the time of Elijah" when "there was a severe famine over all the land," there were "many widows in Israel," but the prophet went only to "a [Gentile] widow at Zarephath in Sidon." Likewise, there were many lepers in Israel, yet "none of them was cleansed except Naaman the Syrian." Luke says that on hearing this, "all in the synagogue were filled with rage." They rose up, drove Jesus "out of the town," and were ready to "throw him off the cliff." Welcoming the outsider, both then and now, is controversial, difficult, and dangerous, yet it is intrinsic to the Jesus Story.

In the earliest churches, the "inclusion of the Gentiles," as shaped by the Apostle Paul, was surely one of the most divisive, radical, and grace-filled ideas and actions in the history of Christianity. Opposition was strong, especially since, as one scholar comments, "Gentiles ate impure substances, and came into regular contact with impure substances, and—what is worse—committed idolatry and defiling sexual acts."[6] Yet in Acts 10, Peter the Apostle has a vision in which he learns, "What God has made clean, you must not call profane" (10:15 NRSV). Shortly thereafter, he is summoned by the Spirit to the home of Cornelius, a Gentile. On arrival, Peter declares, "You yourselves know that it is unlawful for a Jew to associate with or to visit a Gentile; but God has shown me that I should not call anyone profane or unclean" (10:33 NRSV). Then, in Galatians 2, Paul says that in Antioch, Peter hung out with the Gentiles until certain Jewish Christians arrived, and "he drew back and kept himself separate for fear of the circumcision faction. And the other Jews joined him in this hypocrisy…" (Gal 2:12-13 NRSV).

In the early 1980s, I sat in on a workshop at a missions conference conducted at the theological seminary where I was then teaching. The workshop was led by a prominent retired Baptist missionary whom I had heard as a teenager. In the course of her presentation, she asserted that if "God were in control" in the USA, then the government would be compelled to "execute homosexuals, adulterous couples, and rebellious children." Knowing certain students in the room, I realized that had that been the case, a considerable number of the students would surely have been long gone. A professorial colleague inquired of the missionary, "But what about the prodigal son?" She looked at both of us and declared, "You boys don't believe the Bible, do you?"

The missionary's comment and the essays in this book remind us of how often in the church's history Christians have acted punitively against people and movements deemed heretical or in some way outside the boundaries of the gospel—claiming biblical support for fighting holy wars, beheading heretics, drowning witches, keeping slaves, and enforcing conversion therapy. Only after decades, sometimes centuries, did we finally realize that what we thought to be "biblical" turned out not to be gospel. We might reflect on that as we read this important and timely text.

## Notes

[1] Frederick Buechner, *The Sacred Journey* (San Francisco: Harper & Row, Publishers, 1982), 58.

[2] John E. Fortunato, *Embracing the Exile* (San Francisco: Harper & Row, Publishers, 1982), 35.

[3] Marina Pitofsky, "America is changing how it views accepting gay and lesbian people, new poll reveals," *USA Today*, February 2, 2022.

[4] Andrew Demillo, "Other States are Copying Florida's Don't Say Gay Laws," Washington Post, March 23, 2023; William Wan, "Kentucky Legislature Passes Anti Trans Law, Overriding Governor's Veto," *Washington Post*, March 30, 2023; Mark Wingfield," Jacksonville church isn't the only SBC congregation requiring members to affirm statements on homosexuality," Baptist News Global, February 17, 2023.

[5] Cody J. Sanders, *Queer Lessons for Churches on the Straight and Narrow* (Macon, GA: Faithlab, 2013), 18.

[6] Jonathan Klawans, "Notions of Gentile Impurity in Ancient Judaism," *Association for Jewish Studies* 20, no. 2 (1995): 286.

# Chapter 1

# The Perils of Purple Churches

### Rev. Dr. Jake Hall

*Rev. Dr. Jake Hall is an experienced baptist pastor, nonprofit leader, and willing conspirator for justice in Macon, Georgia, where he serves as Executive Director of United to End Homelessness.*

They call themselves "purple" churches.

That description has nothing to do with the decor of the church, the hue of the drapes, or the shade of the carpet. This is a reference to the political ideologies in the pews.

Purple churches like to think of themselves as a big tent where all are welcome. The idea is that such a church can be a place where the polarized opposites of liberal and conservative, Republican and Democrat, can come together. I should know; I have served various shades of purple churches throughout my career as a pastor, from those who are light lavender in suburban settings to the deep plum color of a deeply divided body.

This blending of opposing political ideologies professes an equal mixing of red and blue. By identifying as "purple," institutions are signaling that they are not aligned exclusively with one political ideology or party, and strive to represent a more centrist position that is open to diverse perspectives. The term "purple" has been used in this way in a variety of contexts, including politics, media, and education.

In the United States, the term "purple state" is often used to describe states that are politically competitive, a roughly equal number of voters who identify as Democrats or Republicans. Purple could be a good thing. It sounds positive, doesn't it? Theologically, at its best, it represents the subordination of political ideologies in order to bow to a more determinative identity in Christ.

I have just never actually seen it work out that way. Functionally, it doesn't remove partisan concerns from the life of a congregation so much as it denies engaging in any issues that could raise the ire of either side of the congregation's badly formed binary body politic.

The only way that purple churches can exist is by holding a delicate balance, often in silence. Pastors of these congregations must always know how far they can push the church in matters of social justice without crossing a line that will land them in trouble with one constituency or another. In purple churches, there are certain topics that are simply off-limits. Often, these topics are issues around sexuality, gender, race, social justice, immigration, trauma, and gun control. If you ask them, they will tell you. Every pastor who serves a purple church knows what topics will upset the fragile equilibrium.

Purple churches create a facade of diversity by suppressing, silencing, or avoiding any issue or person that, by their existence, might challenge the perceived peace. You disturb that peace to your own peril. Leadership frameworks that protect this culture commit a kind of shared idolatry that worships the perceived unity of most church members to the exclusion of people whose presence may disquiet the peace.

Edwin Friedman was an American family therapist strongly influenced by Bowen Family Systems Theory. Friedman emphasized the role of leadership and emotional maturity in creating healthy family systems and organizations. Families operate as emotional systems, he said, with each member's behavior and emotions impacting the behavior and emotions of the other members.

Unhealthy family systems lack adaptation, resilience, and, dare I say, grace. Change in these brittle systems feels like death. Once equilibrium has been achieved, church stakeholders will commit all sorts of sins in order to avoid the pain and confusion of a disquieted family system. They will discriminate against women in ministry, ignore cries for racial justice, pacify themselves with devotional pablum, wear themselves out with chronic if ineffective charity, and distract themselves with the repetitive nostalgia of the Wednesday night supper. All the while they will exclude those who can't fit nicely into the contrived peace of red and blue in a black and white congregation. This bloodless gospel disengages from the very fierce theological proclamation of justice the world needs in areas of personhood, racial equity, gender equality, and matters of economic justice.

Ministers who manage a congregation's emotional system in this way are not practicing pastoral ministry. This is chaplaincy to the status quo. These are the duties of the concierge at the country club or the cruise director on the latest and largest Royal Caribbean liner. This is not prophetic, pastoral ministry but something closer to hospice chaplaincy for a congregation's former relevance.

A key to health in a complex congregational system for Friedman was his concept of "differentiation." This refers to the ability of individuals to separate their own emotions and behavior from those of others in the system. Highly differentiated individuals are able to maintain a sense of self and make decisions based on their own values, rather than being swayed by the emotions and expectations of others.

Purple churches exist not by differentiation but through codependency and enmeshment. This shared commitment to equilibrium must be enforced by a set of postures and practices that protect purple churches from disquieting thoughts and punish those who may disturb the balance. Pastors who are called to churches with enmeshed cultures "succeed" by preaching devotional sermons that inspire the comfortable and disquiet no one.

What happens when forces outside the congregation affect the ability of the system to hold this fragile state of cheap peace? Over the past decade, political polarization, the pandemic, and evolving discourse around justice has exposed the cowardice and irrelevance of these postures and the damage they inflict on the body of Christ.

The Supreme Court decision of Obergefell v. Hodges revealed just how much I had accepted and protected this lie as a pastor and allowed it to shape my own practice of ministry and the church systems in which I worked. In 2015, the Supreme Court decided on the grounds of the fourteenth amendment that same-sex marriage was legal under the equal protection clause and that no state should deny or deprive any person of life or liberty in this way.

This shifting paradigm began to raise the anxiety in churches who avoided such "political" matters. Managing this anxiety and pacifying the power brokers in a delicate balancing act, I told myself, was the price of being a successful pastor. It was a lie I chose to believe, until my excuses came crashing down.

Focusing on the centrality of the gospel does not demand ignoring the historic inequities of race or the exclusion of our LGBTQ+ siblings. The gospel demands engaging these inequities. Neutrality when it comes to systemic abuse, inequity, and exclusion are not secondary concerns of the gospel. Bishop Desmond Tutu once said, "If you are neutral in situations of injustice, you have chosen the side of the oppressor. If an elephant has its foot on the tail of a mouse and you say that you are neutral, the mouse will not appreciate your neutrality." Neutrality is not peace. Tolerance is merely veiled contempt. Silence is not love.

Words matter when it comes to community. "Language is never innocent." This quote, which appears in the introduction to *Mythologies*, is a key idea that underpins Roland Barthes's concept of language. Language is always loaded with cultural and ideological meaning. For example, preaching out loud that "everyone is welcome at our church" is a statement that many churches make. Some actually mean it, and others say it even if they know that not every body truly counts as part of everybody when the statement is uttered.

Pastors who proclaim "all are welcome here" but know that their congregations do not wholly acknowledge the priestly calling, personhood, or struggle of people of color, women, or members of the LGBTQ+ community tell a half-truth and a whole lie in order to make themselves and their congregations remain connected in a blind and brittle "peace."

I know because I have offered that kind of welcome. And I knew that it wasn't really true, yet.

Until one experience shook me out of my comfortable privilege and caused all of my pragmatic and political reasons of avoidance and waiting to fall away. It changed the way I preached, taught, led, advocated, and bore witness in matters of justice. It revealed my own complacency and provoked confession and a commitment to repentance.

I had to come to terms with my sinfulness in not jeopardizing my pastoral capital, influence, or even my job in my avoidance of advocating for LGBTQ+ people. I am ashamed it took so long.

Two weeks after the Obergefell decision in June 2015, I received a message from a couple. These two wanted to get married on the church's campus. They were ready to say yes to the next phase of their life, and given that the Supreme Court had created space for marriage equality, they wanted space to get married at the church in eight weeks.

My knee-jerk reaction was fear. Fear leads to self-protection more than self-sacrifice. Fear isn't truly Christ-like. We remember that Jesus kept telling everyone not to be afraid. Yet I felt I had to take responsibility for managing the church's anxiety around this issue. I also knew instinctively that it was now impossible to hold on to the purple peace without disturbing the church body.

Churches will commit all manner of lesser evils to protect their fragile collective sense of self, theology be damned. They will alienate people; they will run off ministers and radically redefine their church life to protect their control over who is allowed in and who is allowed to lead.

I knew where my personal convictions were on whether these two could be married on the church campus, but I also knew that this was something that the church simply didn't want to talk about. Honestly, I was afraid. I did not know how to navigate the theological or political tensions on the other side of unleashing this issue to the congregation. I had a difficult time reconciling my personal convictions of inclusion with the church's de facto practice of don't ask and don't tell; everything is fine; let's just not talk about it.

I knew it would be an explosive issue, and I deluded myself into doing what I perceived to be the "greater good" of the church at the time. I had bought into a pragmatic, if not theological, argument that the church couldn't handle a difficult conversation about inclusion without fracturing the membership, dashing the budget, booting the pastor, or all of the above. I told myself the safe way was the faithful way, but for whom was it safe?

I believed the idea that losing too many members was like losing clients in a business. I should likewise avoid these topics so as not to affect the bottom line of the budget at the end of the year. I worried about the adage from a deacon about how to measure success in this church: "by butts in seats and profit at the end of the year." But attendance and profit are not theological measures of faithfulness, nor are they congregational metrics of spiritual maturity. Our language is never innocent, and the words I was using to frame my thoughts were born out of consumerism and not Christianity.

It seemed like the world was lurching forward around us. So many churches were realizing that their practices around sexuality and gender were harmful to human psyches and claims of belovedness. This couple did not want to become the fulcrum on which our church made a decision, and yet they wanted a decision.

I didn't want to be the fulcrum on which the church made this decision either. I decided to poll the deacons in private conversations, and then I checked in with the deacon officers about where the church stood at that moment in time. "Are we ready?" I asked. "Not yet," was the resounding answer.

I talked with the couple and informed them that this church was not ready to decide on how to decide about whether or not to host their wedding on campus. My wife and I were invited to their wedding, which took place in their backyard. It was a beautiful ceremony, with deep joy. We were honored to attend, and we celebrated their union. My heart grieved knowing I had participated in what I framed at the time as the right wrong decision.

It was the pragmatic thing to do, I believed. This patience will pay off, I told myself. Handling a congregational conversation about sexuality and LGBTQ+ inclusion in haste could jeopardize the church actually achieving full inclusion, I believed. I also knew I had shredded my own convictions for the church's perceived needs of an easy sense of itself.

Months later, I was in a meeting in my office with the newlywed couple. They were in tears fueled by pain and anger. Additional staff was there, and we struggled to articulate a response. I knew the time had come for honest confession. I had wronged them. I had protected the wrong thing and not the right people.

I looked them in the eyes and apologized for the pain and my participation in it. I knew that I had not followed my own convictions. I apologized because by seeking equilibrium in the church I had not done my duty to lead in love as I should, and I pledged to them that it would be the last time I shredded my conviction on this issue. I named that it was unacceptable for this couple to be personally accepted by the pastor and corporately ignored by the church. They looked in my eyes and we cried together. It was one of the holiest moments in my ministry.

I looked around and saw the purple bruises that purple pastoring had wrought. I looked in the mirror and I saw a purple pastor servicing a purple church. Protecting the church from difficult conversations did not advance the kingdom of God;

it preserved a pale version of the church that was dismissive of beloved children of God in their midst and the real needs of folks outside the inner circle of the church.

My protections of their peaceful easy feelings of togetherness offered very little to making this group of people more like Christ. Instead, it just reinforced the experience of church as a club whose membership policies were restrictive and exclusive. It had the function of making them more like each other. Like many of the other writers in this book, I didn't know what to do, but I knew that I had to change. So I began to embody that change.

The formal church structures may not have been ready to begin the conversation. But when are we ever ready? I'm not sure there's ever a time in which a church is eager and ready to change from whatever the status quo has become into whatever transformative thing God may have in store. I could no longer embody neutrality as a pastor—not in my preaching, not in my service, not in the liturgy, and not in my ministry bearing witness in our city. We began to embody, acknowledge, and organically change by our actions if not by a formal articulation in our constitution, bylaws, policies, and procedures. I didn't need Robert's Rules of Order or a church vote to begin to do the right thing.

What if Barthes was right? We, as a congregation, had never formally excluded anyone. We proclaimed that "all are welcome." What if I simply began leading as if that were wholly true? Acting and performing that word of welcome until we understood it more fully and were more fully known. "Language is never innocent." Could it now be used to aid and abet a progressive future instead of policing and protecting a regressive past?

I decided to allow love to overtake the fear I held.

This organic and embodied approach sought to honor the lives of the LGBTQ+ people in our midst while also avoiding the spectacle of a vote. Truthfully acknowledging the wholeness and holiness of LGBTQ+ people in our congregation, we published wedding anniversaries in the bulletin. We invited our LGBTQ+ members and attenders to wholly participate in committee leadership and recruited them for worship leadership and directing choirs. In the worship bulletin bio, we listed our LGBTQ+ couples in the same way as other heterosexual couples and families, naming their hobbies and committee leadership. We engaged in hard conversations about place and race. It was a small and organic step toward embodying the welcome of Christ for all people in new ways for this congregation.

We were learning that we didn't know the invisible limits we had placed on church participation. I made an agreement with myself and with God that day that I would no longer break my own convictions for the sake of a congregation's fear. I started learning more about what it meant to be an ally and then an advocate. This happened not just in personal relationships within my sphere, but corporately. I began to speak more openly and to advocate for civil rights for all people in our community. I followed the call of Christ to care for all people and crafted moments of advocacy in the community, even knowing that my purple congregation might be listening and that it could earn me a purple heart.

I had been complicit, and now it was time to conspire for change. For a while it was beautiful. We got to see the new growth happening in our congregation without having to facilitate that change by way of called conferences and garish votes. People from diverse backgrounds began to attend worship. Our leadership structure and deacon board members began to embody that change too, as new people were nominated and elected to serve in leadership.

Purple churches can be perilous places. The dynamics that keep things polite can also be employed to course correct when peace is disturbed for any reason. The temperature of political polarization hit new highs in the time leading up to 2016 and beyond. I believe so many purple churches felt it. I know mine did.

Suddenly, there was a sense of desperation to protect the fragile peace against off-limits topics. Immigration, controversies about the Trump presidency, systemic racism, the reckoning of #metoo, as well as needs from the LGBTQ+ community all simmered on the surface. Then came the COVID-19 pandemic.

The pandemic created new afflictions in congregations who were once a little more open to these conversations. A kind of congregational compression syndrome set in. The pockets of communication that could usually be tempered by sharing communion on Sunday mornings and meals around the table on Wednesday nights were sealed off from one another. We didn't get to sit and chat. When we did engage, there was more heat than light on a host of issues. Coming out of 2021, I know of so many pastors who were in a firestorm of conflict due to the complex pressures of the pandemic, church politics, and dysfunction.

The pandemic changed things. We know that. Churches were disappointed all the time, and issues of race and sexuality disturbed the equilibrium they believed kept the church happy. But the pandemic also revealed things. Churches would do anything to return to their perceived equilibrium.

Entering into the work of change—the work of understanding, listening, empathy, and seeing belovedness—has never come easily for the church, historically. It won't be easy for us now. But easy is not the goal.

If you ever hear a congregation describe themselves as a "purple church," you might need to beware. You might run, and don't look back. You might ask, how exactly is that color formed, and how is it protected?

What happens if the color changes? What happens if, instead of equal amounts of red and blue, neatly contained and never disrupted, they begin to spill out and spill all over the pews and into the lives of the people who have chosen to quietly abide by the right wrong choices?

What happens when people look each other in the eyes and confess the ways they have dismissed and hurt one another? What happens when they realize that the time has come never again to choose silence, or politeness, or avoidance? What happens when ministers confess and claim that purple is not enough? What happens when they begin to invite the beautiful, wonderful, gifted people who come near to your congregation to offer up their whole selves for the kindom of God?

What happens? Our true colors are revealed.

## Chapter 2

# On Reading Scripture—and Our Neighbors—Well

### Rev. Dr. Preston Clegg

*Rev. Dr. Preston Clegg is Pastor of Second Baptist Church in Little Rock, Arkansas.*

Every Sunday, I leave my congregation—Second Baptist Church in Downtown Little Rock—with the same benediction: "As you go, go and love God with all your heart, soul, mind, and strength. And love your neighbor as yourself. Do so as if it's the most important thing in all the world…because it is."

Obviously, this benediction emphasizes the primacy of the Great Commandment in our faith. In Jesus' eyes, this is the beginning motivation and final measure of our faith. There is nothing more important than loving God and neighbor.

The author of the Gospel of Matthew adds that "on these two commandments hang all the law and the prophets" (22:40, NRSV). In other words, these commandments aren't just the emotive center and affective impetus of our faith; they are also the hermeneutical key to reading the scriptures well. The law and prophets move on these commands like a door "hangs" on its hinges. The book of Leviticus, the prophet Nahum, and even the rugged Amos have something to teach us about the way we love God and neighbor. To engage Scripture in such a way that it leads us away from love is to read it wrongly; to engage Scripture in such a way that it leads us into deeper, broader, richer love is to read it as Jesus read it.

My favorite of the "Great Commandment texts," however, stems from the Gospel of Luke, chapter 10. In this text, a lawyer asks Jesus about eternal life. Jesus responds, "What is written in the law? How do you read it?" (v. 26, NIV). Again, this is a hermeneutical question that every Bible reader asks every time they open a biblical text, even at a subconscious level. How do I read this? What did this text mean then, and what does it mean today? Within this single question—"How do you read it?"—lies the entire field of biblical interpretation in a nutshell.

But because this lawyer is familiar with the Hebrew law, he responds to Jesus' question in language that is eerily similar to what Jesus says in the other Gospels: "'Love the Lord your God with all your heart and with all your soul and with all your strength and with all your mind' and, 'Love your neighbor as yourself'" (10:27, NIV). In Luke, the great commandments are spoken on the lips of this lawyer, not Jesus.

Jesus says, "Do this and you will live" (v. 28 NIV). The man responds, "And who is my neighbor?" (v. 29 NIV). In response, Jesus tells the famed tale of the Good Samaritan, an ostracized other who acts with compassion and love towards another person in grave need.

A conversation that begins with the hermeneutical question "How do you read it?" quickly gives way to a question of relational commitment, "Who is my neighbor?"

"How do you read it?" … "Who is my neighbor?'
"How do you read it?" … "Who is my neighbor?"
"How do you read it?" … "Who is my neighbor?"

Those two questions dance together, debate with each other, inform each other, and enrich each other. The one has everything to do with the other, and improving the one improves the other by sheer relationship.

This hermeneutical lesson from the Gospel of Luke clearly guided the decisions of the early church in Luke's second volume, the book of Acts. The early church, following Jesus' hermeneutical trajectory, welcomed Gentiles into the early Christian movement, and they welcomed them as Gentiles rather than demanding that they become culturally Jewish before joining the movement. The early church did not mandate circumcision, even though this move was contrary to the "plain reading of Scripture" on that matter. The early church followed the leading of the Spirit and the primacy of love as the fount of wisdom and discernment on Gentile inclusion into the body of Christ. In retrospect today, we understand that move to be most consonant with the way of Christ and faithful to the gospel of Jesus, but many in that context saw it as a move that diluted the holiness of God's people and relaxed the standards of Holy Scripture. Within the biblical canon, not outside of it, we see the trajectory of love as the most faithful hermeneutical posture. They opened the Scriptures in such a way that the Scriptures opened their hearts, minds, and doors.

At Second Baptist Church, we've learned that we're not reading our Scriptures rightly if we're loving our neighbors poorly, especially those neighbors who have been categorized as socially "other." Likewise, our love for neighbors is enriched and given life and vitality by the wisdom of the Scriptures, mined from a right heart and mind.

In 1957, Second Baptist Church advocated for the integration of Little Rock Central High School amid national attention surrounding the crisis. The church did so as a predominately and historically white Baptist church because it felt a sense of love's compulsion toward justice, equity, and inclusion. At the same time, other ministers and other churches were using scriptural verses—primarily those about law and order—to support the segregation of the races in schools. But that biblical hermeneutic was not born of love; it was born of a desire to suppress the neighbor. When one picks up a Bible with a wrong heart, it's difficult to interpret it with a right mind.

The church paid a steep price for this call for justice, losing both people who disagreed with the stance and the money those people gave to support the ministry. However, the compulsion of love prevailed. In retrospection, we celebrate that decision of our forebears. Today, we see so clearly their courage, faithfulness, and gospel-shaped conscience. But in that moment, this move was highly debated and hotly contested, and many of the fiercest opponents of integration had a Bible in hand.

In the same way, Second Baptist Church began ordaining female deacons in the 1970s, just as the fundamentalist takeover of the Southern Baptist Convention began to center its attention on women in ministry as a proxy issue for biblical fidelity. Fundamentalists appealed to certain biblical texts that seemed to clearly denounce and prohibit women in leadership. But again, the hermeneutical primacy of love led us to a more just, equitable, and inclusive posture. Our decision to ordain women made us a unique congregation in Arkansas, with precious few Baptist churches joining us in that conviction. For decades now, women have been leading Second Baptist Church at every level, using their gifts and graces for the good of the church and the furtherance of God's reign.

This historical and theological trajectory was once again our guiding light in 2014, when the church decided to enter an intentional discernment process about our inclusion of LGTBQ people in our midst. During this process, we studied the Scriptures more—not less—trying to understand the apparently clear biblical witness on these matters. We also studied the science, history, psychology, and medical wisdom on this subject so that we understood—as much as possible—the hardships and travails of our LGBTQ+ neighbors.

For many people, the "issue" of LGBTQ+ inclusion is simple because they believe the biblical witness is simple. In just this way, those who advocated for the enslavement of humans and those who forbade women in leadership had "clear readings of the biblical text" in their favor. But these readings flew in the face of the overarching biblical trajectory, and they set the reader in a combative posture toward their neighbor. The "clear and simple" reading of a biblical text is not always the best and most faithful reading, especially when it seems to contradict what love would do rather than inform it.

Furthermore, LGBTQ+ "matters" are primarily about LGBTQ+ people. To think of this debate as being over an issue casts many real human beings into the ditch rather than lifting them out, the exact opposite of the Samaritan impulse.

Surely love centers the person, the beloved, and does not make of them an "issue" or a "matter." When discussing human sexuality, we're discussing people who bear the image of God. Only the utmost reverence and care is due that conversation, and surely those who are most impacted by the decisions should have the most significant say in the result.

In 2018, Second Baptist voted to become a fully affirming church of LGBTQ+ folks. They are privy to the benefits of our communal life together and also held to the expectations of that same life. Since that time, LGBTQ+ people have been welcomed to every aspect of church leadership including deacons, support staff, pastoral staff, and Sunday school teachers. These LGBTQ+ folks are the better for their place in the church, but the church is better for it all the more. Often, we can see how LGBTQ+ folks need the church, but we fail to realize how much the church needs LGBTQ+ people. Remember, in the parable of the Good Samaritan, it's the Samaritan who helps the vulnerable man in the ditch; it's not that the Samaritan is the person in the ditch.

To be clear, we did not arrive at this place of affirmation by neglecting the Scriptures but by engaging them. We did not study the Bible less during this process, but more, and we surrounded this Bible study with contextual studies of sexuality in the ancient world, how same-sex attraction and behavior was understood and expressed in Greco-Roman cities such as Corinth and Ephesus, the preponderance of gross sexual abuse saturating those sexual expressions, and the way certain biblical texts were translated throughout history. Then, we considered how the ancient expressions of same-sex relationships compared and contrasted with those of our day. Thus, we did not sidestep the Scriptures but engaged them at their heart.

The difference for us, however, was not an increase in quantity of biblical study but a different quality of biblical study, one determined to love the LGBTQ+ "other" the best, wisest, and most faithful way we could. We did not seek to merely inform our minds on the topic but also to transform our attitudes towards the people.

I learned several lessons during this process. First of all, I learned that conversations about sexuality are first and foremost conversations about shame. The word "sin" is not mentioned once in the Adam and Eve narrative of Genesis 3, but the primal "fall" of the patriarch and matriarch is laced with shame. They cover themselves from God and from each other. A similar impulse saturates conversations about sexuality, regardless of the nature of one's sexuality. Sex is an inherently vulnerable act, and therefore it is laced with both holiness and shame. Helping folks redeem their shame is essential work in this conversation.

Most LGBTQ+ folks have been ostracized from one community or another, often in the name of God, therefore making them utterly vulnerable in a way that straight and cisgender people can barely imagine. Traditionalists—at least those who are willing to critically engage this issue—have to wrestle with the notion that they've been misguided about sexual matters for some time. Those who have changed their minds on the issue entertain the possibility that they were wrongheaded to do so. Thus, no camp in this conversation is safe from feelings of shame, and walking with people to a place of inclusion demands pastoral assistance to process and redeem the shame we all feel. Everyone is covering their loins—and their hearts—for fear that they will be hurt, wrong, or exposed. Walking tenderly with people, but being guided convictionally, is the pastoral sweet spot of this work.

I believe Second Baptist's history of inclusion paved the way for this work of processing shame. During the civil rights movement, white people in this country were forced to look at grave injustices and their complicity in them. They were forced to deal with the harsh reality that, while racism had distorted the humanity of Black folks by seeking to treat them as something less than human, it had also distorted the humanity of white folks by seeking to treat them as something more than human. And while patriarchy creates suffering for women, it also twists our expectations of males. Everyone is the lesser because of it. In the same way, the oppression of LGBTQ+ people does not merely hurt LGBTQ+ people (though it does hinder them primarily); it also robs all people of the beautiful diversity of God's creation and the church of wisdom, gifts, and graces it does not have otherwise. The sins of homophobia traffic in the same shame as those of racism, sexism, and classism, and one of the most significant ministries of the church in this arena is helping people—*all* people—process and transform their contingent shame.

Second, I've realized that what people are talking about is rarely what people are talking about. What I mean is that you're rarely talking about a thing in and of itself, but most often the concern is some corollary issue. When discussing LGBTQ+ folks' relationship with the church, people are also calculating whom the church could lose or gain in the process, the potent impact on the church budget, potential ramifications of serving in other spheres of belonging like businesses and boards, how other people—like close family—will respond, the response of organizational partners, and many other concerns. Thus, many find it difficult to center themselves on the cause of discernment because they are already calculating the costs and benefits of the journey. But there are times in life to put away the calculators and do what's right. I believe good leaders recognize that they are responsible for their organizations, and good pastors recognize that they are stewarding churches. Thus, the organizational metrics matter and should be considered, but they must not override the very identity of the church. What does it matter if a church gains or retains money and people if it loses its own soul?

Third, in matters of inclusion, most people don't have convictions; they have assumptions disguised as convictions. These assumptions have not been critically engaged. Another perspective has not been considered. The "belief" has not been held up to the light in order to assess its faithfulness. This is especially true when discerning sexuality, something that is experienced at the visceral level more than the rational one. I assume that no one taught you, dear reader, to whom you should be attracted, and I assume you didn't discover your repulsions by reading them in a book. This is a hard saying, I know, but most people's sexual ethic is simply their attractions and/or repulsions covered in a thin veneer of religious sentiment. The sexual ethic of most people has all the heat of a conviction but all the light of an assumption. Therefore, confronting an ethic of exclusion is often an attempt to transform someone's primal urges—both attractions and repulsions. It's profoundly difficult to reason someone out of impulses they urged their way into. It's profoundly difficult to "think" someone out of repulsions they "felt" their way into. It's profoundly difficult to theologize someone out of positions they sexualized their way into. In short, the best theological arguments cannot compensate for a lack of spiritual formation at the deepest levels of one's being.

For all these reasons, stretching the brain of another person without tending the soul of that person is not only pastoral malpractice but is also ultimately ineffectual. Transforming a person in these matters demands an address of the entire person. Deep-seated fears, anxiety, and hopes are tied up in the inclusion of LGBTQ+ people in the church. Personally, I'm skeptical that theological shifts alone will see us forward. We need wholesale spiritual transformation and holistic soul care. Nothing short of that will suffice.

But glory be to God! The church was created to be the perfect place for this inclusion and justice. In a great irony, the institution that many associate with being racist, sexist, and homophobic was formed to be just the opposite of those sins. The church is the one community in the world who believes the greatest truth is love and who holds that one can't think rightly as long as that same one is loving wrongly. The church is where our sacred texts remind us that people are sacred too, even more sacred than our texts. The church is where our baptismal identity of divine belovedness takes precedence and informs all the other aspects of our identity. The church, which has gotten so many things wrong over the centuries and over the last few years, can be the place that models true repentance and restoration.

While this journey of inclusion has been a difficult one for Second Baptist, it has also been a holy one, full of wonder and awe. This journey has humbled us and made us bolder and more convictional at the same time. At this point, in the clarity of retrospection, we wouldn't trade this journey for anything.

"How do you read it?" … "Who is my neighbor?"

As long as those two questions are dancing together, we intend to be moving our feet, hands, and lives to the rhythm. I hope you'll hear that music in your community as well. When you do, I hope you'll dance too.

As you finish this essay, go and love God with all that you are—your heart, soul, mind, and strength. And love your neighbor as yourself. Do so as if it's the most important thing in all the world…because it is.

# Chapter 3

# Catharsis in Communion

### Rev. Dr. Jay Hogewood

*Rev. Dr. Jay Hogewood serves as Senior Pastor of Rayne Memorial United Methodist Church in New Orleans, Louisiana.*

Lunch was proceeding just fine. We picked a North Dallas location between his office and the church where I served. The hum of importance and busyness heaved in my head. The atrium cafe was lovely—airy and filled with light. Clinking forks to plates filled my ears. My lunch date, a longtime church member, was important to me for more than just his longevity at our large Southern Baptist congregation. He was passionate about the ministry of Jesus and had the gifts and graces to show it. He was a leader in our church's single adult ministry, and for good reasons: charismatic and articulate, his witness of Christ's presence and grace made meaning in his life and the life of our active young adult group. The impact of Jesus Christ showed clearly in his relationships and in his very being.

He had kindly invited me to this meal. An agenda had to surface, but I kept wondering when. So far, he was reluctant to reveal it. We broke bread; it was communion.

Deep into our lunch, the swirl of sounds melted to the floor. Finally, I sensed the agenda floating on our horizon. His eyes were the first to show it. I could've heard a pin drop. Silence, then a sip of water. He whispered with some strain, saying, "Jay, I need you to know the truth about me, the truth that I'm gay. I am a homosexual man."

### A Homophobic Minister

My immediate thoughts were, "Who am I that he would break bread with me and then dare to share such brokenness? Who am I that he would open for me a floodgate of questions, considerations, and even my own reformation as a follower of Jesus? And now what? What am I supposed to do? Who am I to deal with such a problem?"

The answer: I was his minister. I was his suddenly shaken, homophobic minister.

## Repentance Begins: Sorting through the Baggage

My perspectives against homosexuality, and against any form of sexual orientation other than *straight* (cis-gendered, nonbinary) were more a culmination of cultural baggage and biblical malformation than thoughtful study or spiritual examination. First, the cultural baggage is easy enough to call out. *Heteronormativity*, to my recollection, was not a word we used but simply a foregone conclusion when I was growing up. As children of the 1970s, Gen Xers like me only knew "gay" as a term of derision, a put-down. Being called "gay Jay" cemented that perspective for me. Friends were quick to chirp out the cutting rhyme for laughs at my expense. A couple of middle school fights were what I hoped could prove not only that I was *not* gay but that I'd throw fists over it too. Add to my personal association with *gay* as an insult the height of the HIV/AIDS crisis, and I can't so much fault my childhood cultural frame as lament it or grieve over it. After all, was anyone I knew in high school or college "openly gay"? No way! Heaven forbid.

First, I lacked any frame of reference for gay and lesbian relationships. I feel it's important for me to say that I had not ever encountered venomous, hate-filled rhetoric about queer relationships (or what we now call LGTBQ+ persons in loving relationships) as such—not from my parents, not from my Baptist pastors in my hometown of Birmingham, not from my Young Life leaders. If ever there was a concept that was simply "in the air I breathed," the idea of *not* being gay and *not* having sex before marriage would count as two parts oxygen. At no point do I recall feeling forced to examine the matter either. You don't inspect the air; you just keep breathing it.

Second, as for Bible and interpretive malformation, the coming out of my congregant to me greeted me at the most fertile time. I was in my second year of seminary at Truett Theological Seminary, Baylor University. To that point in my life, Holy Scripture was more an instruction manual than an inspired narrative. My professors had begun to guide me toward understanding scripture as an overarching storyline with many voices and various perspectives on the journey of God with God's people—history theologized, yet with diverse literary genres and multiple voices over centuries of accumulation; a gumbo of delights, let's call it, where each book of the Bible presents its own flavor, joining with other flavors to form faith, not just inform the mind about rights and wrongs. To that point in my life, I had only known scripture as a rulebook for living.

"If the only tool you have is a hammer, then every problem is a nail," as the saying goes. I wielded the Bible accordingly, hammering down any thought that didn't fit in my tidy interpretive box. There was nothing gentle or close to gracious about my biblical interpretation, particularly toward those whom we now know as loved ones and neighbors and friends within the LGBTQ+ community.

My time at Truett (yes, a *Baptist* seminary) initiated a new understanding of scripture—authoritative for living faithfully in the Way of Jesus, yes, but not inerrant, which is not a word any biblical writer used to describe their writings anyway. My professors, thoughtful and faithful Baptist scholars, dealt graciously with the biblical text, not self-righteously or defensively. They introduced me to a life-giving, faith-forming understanding of the Bible. In turn, they asked me, "Where is the modesty in your epistemology?"

Okay, maybe not in so many words, but that was the implication. I knew what I knew (my epistemology) because the Bible told me so. Clarity—you bet I had plenty of that, alright. Humility—not so much. My professors asked, "How do you know what you know about sacred scripture?" I knew what I knew about scripture because I could read it myself. Not so modest, huh?

I'm sad to confess it: my thoughts and feelings about the Bible were utterly flush with pride. My Truett professors of biblical interpretation were faithfully, graciously opening new ways to see and experience the sacred scripture; because being able to read the words of the Bible in no way guaranteed that I conceptualized the deeper context, the cultural histories of diverse books and various writers of scripture, or the richness of biblical Hebrew, Aramaic, or New Testament Greek. As a result, I had long approached the Bible with a heavy hand, a closed mind, and a seriously prideful spirit.

I had stripped the gospel story of its powerful good news so that all I had left was an oozing wound of guilt, shame, and fear. Basically, it was what amounted to really bad news: guilt about any sexually impure thought; shame about any sexual expression; and fear over disappointing Jesus of the rulebook, Christ of the instruction manual.

## New Horizons

God's gift is that of serendipity—the aligning of events beneficially and fruitfully. That lunch appointment was the first crack in my previously impenetrable self-righteous wall. My congregant's gift of coming out to me represented a beautiful moment of change. What is change if not the root of repentance? I needed to change my perspective about faithful, Christ-following people who also happened to identify as LGBTQ+, and I needed to turn from fear to trust—trusting, loving, caring, Christ-centered interpretations of scripture. Fear annihilates faith; in my case, it was fear over disappointing my narrow conception of God's righteousness or fear about finding other possible interpretations of the Bible. In other words, that gentle soul who sat across from me was not a nail, so maybe it was time for me to surrender my hammer.

At the same time, within that same spring semester, my Greek New Testament professor and my Hebrew Bible professor guided me from my smug certainty to more and more faithful questions. Faith, after all, is not contained in more answers; faith is the liberation to feel loved, even *saved*, through more and more questions within the peace of Christ. Rabbinic texts before Jesus, our Chief Rabbi, showed this to be true. Turning and turning the texts of the Torah, the ancient rabbis aimed not to lock down definite answers but to open up more questions. How much more did Jesus, who taught through confounding parables and inexplicable miracles, welcome his disciples to ask more questions, even as they followed him. "Unless you change and become like little children, you will never enter the kingdom of heaven" (Matthew 18:3, NIV).

## A More Faithful View of Scripture

From a congregant's coming out, I was invited beyond the Other. In this case, homosexuality was embodied, not a distant idea. Right before me sat a lovely, humble, gracious follower of Jesus, who also happened to feel attraction to men. The combination of that lunch date and scriptural study launched my journey toward a more faithful and fruitful understanding of the Bible, particularly its orientation to same-sex relationships. Granted, those verses are very few and far between, which means a hardcore doctrine *against* homosexuality (or any LGBTQ+ persons) felt more and more contrived, more artificial, to what scripture means for any of us as its interpreters.

By the grace of Jesus Christ, I was finally ready to see a person for who he was and as someone in whom God delighted. Of course, this didn't happen in a moment, though that would have been much easier. It took many more months, even years, up to this moment in my life as a minister. Not until my last semester of seminary did I come to the point of a bit more modesty in my epistemology: I finally admitted that the biblical texts I used as my hammer were insufficient proofs to cancel same-sex relationships formed in loving, faithful, mutual, affectionate contexts. I confessed that I needed more grace to interpret scripture faithfully, not more certainty.

The journey does continue. After my MDiv I completed a PhD in Hebrew Bible/Theological Hermeneutics. I share that because I think much of my desire to learn more of the biblical text was driven not just by information but by my need for more formation by the Holy Spirit through deep engagement in God's Word. While my studies over those seven years did not focus on human sexuality within the Bible, I did benefit from wonderful scholars at Hebrew Union College and then Texas Christian University (Brite Divinity School) who passionately and faithfully showed me the depth of scripture's history of interpretation, as well as approaches to the Bible that were not just more thoughtful but more fruitful for preaching and teaching. Along the way, I have more fully repented of my harsh and hurtful views about loving relationships that happened to be same-sex. Maybe I'm finally finding more modesty in epistemology.

## And as for *Those* Passages

Because biblical interpretation is my academic background and the heartbeat of my faith, I want to be careful here. To work through each piece of scant textual evidence concerning same-sex relationships or sexual activity is not my purpose; that work, while extremely important, falls outside the scope of this effort. I will report that I am delighted and humbled to have crossed the paths of numerous biblical scholars who have done this faithful work. Mark Achtemeier's work (*The Bible's Yes to Same-Sex Marriage: An Evangelical's Change of Heart*, WJK: Louisville, 2014) represents a beautifully faithful and rigorous reading of the so-called "clobber texts" related to what we now know as oppositional, even violent, to LGBTQ+ identities and orientations. These texts are as follows: Genesis 19:1-29; Judges 19; Leviticus 18:22; 20:13; Jude 5-7; Romans 1:18-27; 1 Corinthians 6:9-10; and 1 Timothy 1:9-10.

First and foremost, it is wise to consider that the term "homosexuality" is less than a generation old and, by definition, unbiblical. Only by the mid-twentieth century did we (English translators of ancient biblical Hebrew and Greek) begin using this unfortunate word. Simply put, no word fits our modern concept of "homosexuality" that arose from the biblical worldview as seen within sacred scripture. No such words exist that translate into "gay, lesbian, queer, bisexual, or transgendered," as we use them in our time. Accordingly, all condemnations of LGBTQ+ persons for their sexual orientation are woefully anachronistic.

Says Achtemeier, "Reflecting on scripture's guidance about sexual matters, I realized that it all seemed to be designed to foster and protect a person's ability to make an all-encompassing gift of self to a beloved partner in Christ-like love and mutuality." When events encourage the promise of such a gift, the scriptures appear to approve of such relationships. Where relationships or situations thwart such a gift of self, biblical mandates forbid them. Achtemeier adds, "For example, the reason sexual relations apart from marriage fall short of God's intention is that they involve only a partial gift of oneself to the other person. The full gift of one's body to the other person is reflected in the form of sexual relations, but the full gift of life and spirit, expressed in the form of promises and commitments, is lacking" (107). Neither promiscuity nor adultery is God's design. Celibacy is the path Jesus chooses. There appears to be a lot of sacred space between the two. A healthy, faithful ethic of sexuality is the choice God gives us.

For far too long, at least within the evangelical movement, these so-called "clobber texts" have missed the mark of gracious and wise biblical interpretation. At best, they are historical markers of ancient cultural taboos within levitical legislation; and at worst, they remind us that rape and abuses of power (or pederasty, where older men sexually abuse younger boys) have always been horrific in the sight of God. Related to my understanding of pastoral ministry, none of these biblical texts offers relevant guidance to what we now understand as same-sex relationships.

## What's to Come?

I am a twice-divorced minister serving as an ordained elder in the United Methodist Church. To this day, I marvel at the decision of godly and faithful people who have the power to appoint me to pastoral ministry in congregations. What an absolute privilege. I am so grateful for those bishops who have granted me the grace to fulfill what I feel is my calling to serve as a pastor. Sadly, our denomination is splintering even as we speak. We are fractured about our authority to marry LGBTQ+ persons and to ordain LGBTQ+ persons. Many of us as elders feel it is high time to follow the Holy Spirit to fully include those who love their partners faithfully, in mutuality, with affection and equanimity. And why wouldn't we want to call out the called, LGBTQ+ persons included? Many others don't feel the same. Biblical authority, some claim, is the sure proof to continue excluding LGBTQ+ Christians from the gift of full participation in the life of the church. Like them, I yield to the full authority of scripture. I simply hold a different interpretation. Same Bible. Same view of authority. Different hermeneutic, diverse interpretive lenses. A select handful of passages does not a doctrine make, for Christ's sake, I'd say. Where there is ambiguity, let grace lead. John Wesley is credited for saying, "In essentials, unity; in non-essentials, liberty; in all things, charity." May it be.

What truly baffles me is that my journey is marked by an unambiguous biblical teaching from Jesus. Jesus himself teaches that divorce is a terrible decision and is qualified by only one event: adultery. Yet here I am. I am a fully connected elder with my orders recognized from my Baptist ordination. Am I the glad token of cultural accommodation? Our denomination would be without quite a few of its pastors if we said, "Divorce is not consistent with Christian faith and practice." Or am I the example of radical grace? The same grace covers us all, no matter how we interpret the authoritative word of sacred scripture.

I desperately want our connection—the UMC—to interpret scripture, particularly about same-sex relationships, with more modesty and Christ-centered grace. I often celebrate that my current context at a church in New Orleans has given me the gift of liberation—to feel encouraged and empowered to preach and teach the full inclusion of LBGTQ+ persons in our community of faith. We are doing our best to do justice, to love kindness, and to walk humbly with our God, as the prophet Micah (6:8) instructs.

The recent work of Cole Arthur Riley rings true for me as a pastor, then as now: "Wonder involves the capacity to be in awe of humanity, even your own. Practicing wonder is a powerful tool against despair. It works the same muscles as hope…believing in goodness and beauty." The more I practice wonder, which must be the opposite of judgment, the more I feel the Spirit's conviction about welcoming all God's children to the Way of Jesus but also into full inclusion in Christ's Body, the church. The past two decades have given me the privilege of seeking more holy wonder—not just believing that all humanity is crafted in God's image but acting on that biblical truth.

Who am I to limit, block, or border the good news of Jesus as well as the inspired richness of the entirety of Holy Scripture? Who am I to say who's worthy of the fullest expression of their humanity along the journey of faith in Christ? Riley cites the wise words of Makoto Fujimara, who teaches: "The most courageous thing we can do as a people is to behold."

I am grateful to say that I want to practice more beholding and less boundary-making. I believe with all my heart that this is the invitation of Jesus in the legacy of his ministry on earth, as well as his Spirit at work in the church. This Jesus, who was surely seen as "queer"—an unmarried, celibate Galilean Jewish man in his late twenties two millennia ago—by his community, was and is the one through whom I want to interpret the diverse texts of the Bible. Who am I to hinder the dynamic movement of Jesus Christ? Who am I to handcuff the Holy Spirit? I have every belief that She would break free, anyway.

# Chapter 4

# Holy Moments and Hallowed Ground

### Rev. Dr. Carol McEntyre

*Rev. Dr. Carol McEntyre serves as Senior Pastor of First Baptist Church in Columbia, Missouri, and is a former moderator of the Cooperative Baptist Fellowship.*

A sobbing teenager in need of comfort and safety changed everything for me.

In 2000, I was a twenty-two-year-old student enrolled in the joint Master of Divinity and Master of Social Work program at Baylor University's Truett Seminary and the Diana Garland School of Social Work. I came to Baylor feeling called to ministry but conflicted about the Bible's teaching on women in ministry. So I was elated when the School of Social Work's field director informed me that it was possible to do my social work internship at a church. For me, interning as a social worker in a congregation setting felt like a great way to dip my toe into ministry.

My potential internship site was Lake Shore Baptist Church in Waco, Texas, and I had heard it was a "liberal" congregation. I asked the field director if the church was officially welcoming and affirming of LGBTQ+ people. I am embarrassed to admit it now, but I didn't want to part of a welcoming and affirming congregation. I was not sure what I believed. Was being gay a sin? That was what I had been taught by my home church, and to be honest, I feared that serving in an affirming church would limit my already constrained postgraduation job prospects. Frankly, I didn't want to deal with LGBTQ+ inclusion, and being cisgender and straight meant I had the privilege to opt out. The field director told me that while Lake Shore was a progressive congregation, the church, as far as she knew, had never made any official statement about LGBTQ+ inclusion.[1] With that assurance, I decided to take the internship at Lake Shore. That decision changed my life in beautiful ways, launching me on a path to pastoral ministry and beginning my journey toward becoming LGBTQ+ affirming.

While at Lake Shore, I worked occasionally with the youth in the church and was asked to serve as a chaperone on a trip to San Antonio. I agreed. Our group stayed in a motel with exterior corridors and cheaply furnished rooms because, of course, it was youth trip! Late one night during that trip, a student named Kelsey knocked on my door and asked if we could talk. We sat on the concrete floor in the corridor with our backs against the wall and legs outstretched. The conversation meandered for a while, and I wondered what Kelsey was trying to tell me. Eventually, they began to cry (Kelsey now uses they/them pronouns).[2] At first, a few tears trickled down their cheek, and later great big sobs erupted from within them. They were crying so hard they could barely speak but eventually blurted out, "I think I might be gay."

I felt the depth of their pain wash over me. They were hurting and reaching out for support. In that moment, I could not bring myself to rebuke or even try to convince them they might not be gay. So I hugged them, held them as they cried, and whispered, "You are going to be okay. You are going to be okay." Afterward, I talked with the youth ministry team about supporting Kelsey, but I don't remember following up with them. While I offered Kelsey a shoulder to cry on, I regret not doing more, especially now that I understand how much gay and lesbian youth suffer. According to The Gay, Lesbian & Straight Education Network (GLSEN), which released a report in 2019[3] on LGBT youth,

- 68.7% of LGBTQ students experienced verbal harassment (e.g., called names or threatened) at school based on sexual orientation, 56.9% based on gender expression, and 53.7% based on gender.
- 25.7% of LGBTQ students were physically harassed (e.g., pushed or shoved) in the past year based on sexual orientation, 21.8% based on gender expression, and 22.2% based on gender.
- 11.0% of LGBTQ students were physically assaulted (e.g., punched, kicked, injured with a weapon) in the past year based on sexual orientation, 9.5% based on gender expression, and 9.3% based on gender.
- LGBTQ youth are more than four times as likely to attempt suicide than their peers, and having at least one accepting adult can reduce the risk of suicide attempts by 40%.[4]

In a recent conversation with Kelsey, I asked them about their experience of growing up queer. Kelsey recounted incidents of harassment and subsequent mental and emotional strain. When they came out to a friend, that person did not maintain confidence, which resulted in Kelsey getting bullied at school. They described struggling throughout their teenage years with depression and suicidal ideation. They believe this trauma could have been avoided if they had come out earlier and had broad support.

I also asked Kelsey about growing up in church. They said the people at Lake Shore were kind, and no one ever said, "Don't be gay." At the same time, the lack of a clear welcoming and affirming policy at Lake Shore meant they were never officially affirmed either. Kelsey said, "The church did not feel like a place of respite," which they indicated would have been helpful. Ambiguity creates an environment of insecurity. When policies are unclear, LGBTQ+ people are uncertain if they are supported and safe. It can also embolden people in the church with negative views to express such ideas in harmful ways.

When Kelsey came out to me, it created a fracture in my theology. Growing up in a conservative independent Baptist church in Tennessee, I was taught homosexuality was a sin. I was also taught not to trust my experience and to ignore the promptings of my heart. Jeremiah 17:9a was a Bible verse I often heard quoted: "The heart is devious above all else; it is perverse" (NRSV). I was told humans have a "sin nature," which would lead us astray. The theology of my youth encouraged me to mistrust my experience with LGBTQ+ people and ignore my heart and instincts. I was taught to submit to the theology handed down to me by people (and by people, of course, I mean straight, white men) who knew more than I did and certainly had authority over me.

Yet when Kelsey came out to me, I felt deep compassion and empathy. Although I would have been afraid to admit it at the time, the experience with Kelsey changed me, and from that point forward, I was welcoming and affirming in my heart. But I still did not know how to approach the "clobber passages"[5] in the Bible or how to talk about inclusion; my theology would take several years to catch up to my heart and experience.

Around the same time I was sitting with Kelsey in the motel corridor in San Antonio, First Baptist Church of Columbia, Missouri, where I now serve as senior pastor, was beginning a journey toward becoming welcoming and affirming. First Baptist was much like Lake Shore, a progressive congregation with an unofficial Don't Ask, Don't Tell practice. First Baptist had a reputation for being a safe place for members of the LGBTQ+ community to worship, and gay and lesbian people were active in the church. Yet the church had no official welcoming policy.

In the early 2000s, state legislatures across the nation were banning "gay marriage." In Missouri, an amendment to the state constitution that would restrict marriage to the "union of one man and one woman" was expected to be on the ballot soon, and gay marriage was a frequent topic of conversation.

Given all that was transpiring in Missouri, Rev. Dr. John Baker, the pastor of First Baptist, Columbia, felt compelled by the Holy Spirit to speak out and support gay and lesbian people who were fighting against the ban. Dr. Baker crafted an inclusivity sermon series based on Romans 15:7, which, depending on your translation, states either "accept" (NIV) or "welcome" (NRSV) "one another, as Christ has welcomed (or accepted) you." Dr. Baker wanted to frame the welcome of LGBTQ+ people within the broader context of supporting other marginalized people. His sermon series focused on Christ's call to welcome all people, especially the marginalized: people with disabilities, women called to ministry, people of color, and, finally, gay and lesbian people. I have heard from many who were members at First Baptist in the early 2000s. They believe that these sermons were some of Baker's best preaching during his thirteen-year tenure.

On the day Dr. Baker preached about gay and lesbian inclusion, he told the congregation, "I started this mental, theological, pastoral journey of understanding not through a symposium, academic texts, or pro-homosexuality literature but through personal relationships with real people needing real help for themselves, their parents, or their children." Through his experience with gay and lesbian people, God led him to reexamine scripture and his theology. Upon doing so, he was surprised by how little the Bible addresses same-sex relationships. He said, "The Ten Commandments don't refer to it. The four Gospels say nothing of it. If Jesus ever said anything about it, we have no record whatsoever." Then, he walked them through the six clobber passages, putting the verses in context and refuting the notion that a plain reading of the Bible clearly indicates same-sex relationships are wrong.

In a conversation with Dr. Baker, he told me that he had to dig deep to preach that sermon because he feared that he might lose his job. The congregation knew the sermon was coming, and the tension in the sanctuary that day was palpable. Some congregants who were gay and lesbian or had LGBTQ+ family members longed to hear a supportive word; others warned him ahead of time that they would walk out the door and never return if he preached full affirmation.

While First Baptist had been a relatively safe place for gay and lesbian people for decades, explicitly identifying inclusion as a value that Christians and the church should uphold proved too much. After Dr. Baker preached the sermon, he did not lose his job, but the church lost about 25 percent of its regular attendees and thousands of dollars in annual income over the next few years. The loss of money was tough and certainly strained the church's ministry, but the severed relationships were more painful. Certainly, LGBTQ+ people in the church felt supported by the pastor and by those who stayed, but the exodus of so many caused much pain.

In the next few years, First Baptist continued to make strides toward inclusion, and the church elected its first gay deacon. Yet the fear of further hemorrhage stalled additional progress, and the church did not adopt an official welcoming policy.

In the years between my graduation from Truett Seminary and my calling as senior pastor of First Baptist Church in Columbia, I continued to be guarded about my openness regarding LGBTQ+ inclusion. I was still trying to figure out my theology. Yet, during these years, I kept meeting LGBTQ+ Christians. The Spirit seemed to be leading me toward these divine encounters. After graduating from seminary, I served as the education minister at an Episcopal Church in Augusta, Georgia, where I met a devoted and thoughtful follower of Jesus who was also a lesbian. She, her partner, and their children actively participated in our church. I witnessed her theological depth and spiritual maturity and asked to hear her story, which she graciously shared with me. Over lunch, she recounted that from an early age she had always had crushes on girls, not boys. As a teenager, she dated boys and tried to convince herself she was not a lesbian. She wondered if she could make a life married to a man. Eventually, she realized that she did not want to live a lie. She wanted to be true to herself, and she came out.

After hearing her story and others, I realized sexual identity is often internally driven.[6] From their earliest recollection, some people desire emotional, romantic, and later physical relationships with those of the same sex. I began to believe some people are born gay and to consider the choices they have. According to the moderate theologians I was reading, a life of celibacy was the only moral option.

In the spring of 2005, I moved to Tennessee to serve as the community minister at First Baptist Church of Knoxville. After a few months in my new church, I called the Episcopal Diocese of East Tennessee to inquire about finding a spiritual director. During my stent in the Episcopal Church in Georgia, I had worked with a spiritual director and learned the value of having someone to serve as my pastor and spiritual confidant. The Diocese in East Tennessee provided a name, and when I met with the person who had been recommended, I discovered much to my surprise that she was a lesbian Episcopal priest.

Early in our journey together, she asked me, "Do you feel comfortable receiving spiritual direction from me?" I honestly was not sure if I felt comfortable, but I did not have the heart to tell her no. So we began to meet for spiritual direction regularly and continued meeting for the next seven years. She shared my mystical bent, and we often talked about our experiences of Jesus. Her spiritual depth and pastoral care proved invaluable.

When my husband and I struggled with infertility, she helped me bear the burden. She was there for me during several miscarriages. I discovered that she and her long-term partner had adopted children. When we finally adopted our son, she celebrated with me, and together we marveled at the joy of gaining children after a long wait. Hearing about her family and her love for her children led me to conclude that compulsory lifelong celibacy is cruel. The gifts of a spouse and now a beautiful baby brought me more joy than anything I had ever experienced. How could I support a theological position that would deny others the chance to have such gifts?

I knew that I could no longer subordinate my intuition and experience with people who are LGBTQ+ to what others insisted I should believe. I could no longer believe that being gay was wrong, nor did I want to condemn people to a life of forced celibacy. I was ready to declare my welcoming and affirming position.

When I was called in 2012 as the senior pastor of First Baptist Church in Columbia, the congregation was still recovering from the earlier loss of attendees and from more recent staff conflict. In my first months, I wanted to provide calm, steady leadership and allow the congregation time to heal.

I did not want to rock the boat too much, too soon.

Less than two years into my tenure at First Baptist, I knew I could not wait much longer to address LGBTQ+ inclusion. The Supreme Court had a case, Obergefell v. Hodges, on its agenda. This case questioned the constitutionality of the bans on same-sex marriage. I was very aware that this court decision would have an impact on our church. About 10 percent of our congregation's members identified as LGBTQ+, and I knew that should the court decide in favor of same-sex marriage, it was a matter of time before I would be asked to officiate a wedding. I was willing to do this, but I wanted my congregation's blessing and support.

I raised the issue with church leadership, and the moment the words were out of my mouth, I could feel the tension. Some council members thought we were already welcoming and affirming, and they did not understand the need for a process. Others, who had been around during the inclusion sermon series, were terrified that we might lose more members, and they did not want conflict. A few thought that being gay was a sin, but they concluded that we are all sinners needing grace, right? We wouldn't highlight another sin, would we? Why focus on this one?

I told the council that this diversity of opinions was precisely why we needed clarity. I explained that churches often say that they welcome people who are LGBTQ+, but welcoming can mean different things. It can mean that an LGBTQ+ person is fully included in the church or simply welcome to come to worship but will never be invited to serve in leadership. It can also mean that LGBTQ+ people are welcome to worship but with the hope that they might someday change.

In addition to a conversion about being welcoming, First Baptist needed to discuss whether our sanctuary could be used for a same-sex wedding and if our clergy were blessed to perform these ceremonies. The church also had never talked about whether we were open to hiring or ordaining a person who was gay, lesbian, or transgender. We needed clarity so that LGBTQ+ people felt safe and so that clergy would know how affirming they could be. In addition, in a world that is often hostile toward people who are LGBTQ+, neutrality is not enough. Our LGBTQ+ friends need affirmation, and they need to know that people are willing to work alongside them to protect their rights, advocate, and help dismantle systems that cause harm.

After several months of discussions, the church council agreed to launch a congregational process. We called the process "Widening Our Welcome." Over the next six months, we studied scripture, listened to the testimonies of gay and lesbian Christians in our church, and heard from counselors. Finally, we invited an affirming theologian to speak.

The six months of conversation were the most stressful time of my tenure at First Baptist. I had many sleepless nights, worried that this conversation would split the church. At the end of this discernment process, the church endorsed a simple statement of LGBTQ+ affirmation, and together we committed to living into our values. Despite our best leadership efforts, the process did not leave us unscathed. Our 5:00 pm worship service, composed of roughly seventy Congolese refugees, decided to leave the church. Some wanted to stay and even expressed their openness to inclusion, but their leadership was resolved to go. They had become beloved church family members and their departure grieved the broader congregation.

Yet this loss was eventually overshadowed by the joy of becoming officially welcoming and affirming. As a congregation, we are free to be clear about our theology, affirmation, and advocacy with LGBTQ+ folks. We believe gay, lesbian, bisexual, and transgender people are God's beloved, created in the image of the divine and worthy of every good gift in this life, including love, sexual intimacy, the chance to be parents, and the opportunity to be a part of an affirming faith community.

Being affirming does not mean we dismiss the Bible. Today, excellent biblical scholarship is available that addresses additional interpretations of the clobber passages.[7] Yet biblical support is not at the heart of why I am now fully welcoming and affirming. Instead, it was my experience with LGBTQ+ people that led me on this journey. Despite what I was taught as a child (not to trust my own wisdom or intuition), I have learned that the Holy Spirit can guide us down paths we never expected. We can choose to read the Bible through an anti-LGBTQ+ lens, or we can trust the experience of gay, lesbian, bisexual, and transgender people. I have chosen the path of trust and so has First Baptist, Columbia. Indeed, we must learn to trust ourselves, the experiences of LGBTQ+ folks, and our faith communities enough to believe that the Holy Spirit still speaks and leads us.

## Notes

[1] Lake Shore officially became a Welcoming and Affirming Congregation through a church vote in 2016.

[2] Today Kelsey identifies as queer and uses they/them pronouns. Queer is an adjective used by some people whose sexual orientation is not exclusively heterosexual or straight. This umbrella term includes

people who have nonbinary, gender-fluid, or gender-nonconforming identities. Once considered a pejorative term, queer has been reclaimed by some LGBTQ+ people to describe themselves; however, it is not a universally accepted term even within the LGBTQ+ community.

[3] Joseph G. Kosciw et al., "The Experiences of Lesbian, Gay, Bisexual, Transgender, and Queer Youth in our Nation's Schools," The 2019 National School Climate Survey, *GLSEN*, 2020. You can read the entire report here: https://www.glsen.org/sites/default/files/2020-10/NSCS-2019-Full-Report_0.pdf.

[4] This statistic cited by the Trevor Project at thetrevorproject.org.

[5] The six or seven verses in the Bible (out of approximately 31,000) that appear to reference same-sex relations are referred to as "clobber passages" because they have been used metaphorically to beat LGBTQ+ folx over the head and shame them.

[6] Today, I understand sexual orientation as being on a spectrum and somewhat fluid, but in my journey toward becoming affirming, the stories of people who knew from an early age they were gay or lesbian were important.

[7] I would suggest Matthew Vines's book *God and the Gay Christian: The Biblical Case in Support of Same-Sex Relationships* or Jim Dant's slim volume *This I Know: A Simple Biblical Defense for LGBTQ Christians*.

# Chapter 5

# A Matter of Life and Death

### Rev. Dr. George A. Mason

*Rev. Dr. George A. Mason is Founder and President of Faith Commons, and serves as Pastor Emeritus at Wilshire Baptist Church in Dallas, Texas.*

It was the most challenging and painful change I led as a pastor. And that is saying something.

In the course of more than thirty-eight years, I led churches to address numerous policies that caused consternation in the two congregations I have served as pastor. These included matters of the scope of participation in the church of divorced persons and women; the political machinations of the fundamentalist takeover of the Southern Baptist Convention and the subsequent formation of the Cooperative Baptist Fellowship; the opening of membership to baptized Christians who had not been previously immersed as believers but were confessional Christians nonetheless; how to deal with the scare of the Ebola virus that had come to our church by way of Liberia; and the challenges of the coronavirus, COVID-19, that all of us experienced in 2020–2021.

Each of these required pastoral courage and sensitivity to people and process in order to navigate the troubled waters of change that many in the congregation simply wished to be avoided in the name of peace. Each time, there was a price to pay for confronting these challenges. In varying degrees, longstanding friendships were tested, members left for other churches, trust was fractured, and yet, on the other side of the turbulence, the church was better and stronger for the experience.

All these things prepared me for the biggest challenge I would face, and yet none of them prepared me adequately for the question of whether lesbian, gay, bisexual, transgender, and queer (LGBTQ+) Christians would be treated equally as members of our church.

Wilshire Baptist Church in Dallas, Texas, is a church with a long history of taking the road less traveled by. When in the course of congregational life it seems that our practices have stifled the Spirit's work among us rather than enabling it, we have examined ourselves, plumbed our tradition, searched the scriptures, and forged new paths that would broaden the participation of our members in the work of the gospel. Because we operate with congregational polity, decisions are made by the members of the local church without dictate from or deference to denominational or associational bodies outside it.

Nonetheless, change is always accompanied by anxiety. The question is whether the anxiety will thwart the possibility of change by sabotaging it before it can take place, or the change will produce a new status quo that better reflects the church's understanding of God's will and way with us.

Church members sometimes look to the church as a sanctuary from the whirlwinds of the world, a place to go where they can be assured that some things never change. There's constant tension for Christians between past and future, continuity and surprise, history and hope. Tradition is shaped by cultural conditioning, scriptural interpretation, and longstanding practices that support strategies of stability. This stands in contrast to a faith animated by the Spirit of the coming reign of God that makes every settled custom provisional and calls us to risk reordering our world to conform to the justice of God.

Pastors feel the same tug of war in their souls that members feel. We live with concern for the institution we inherited, which includes the desire to honor the faithfulness of those who have gone before us and not demonize them while we question the spiritual propriety of continuing certain policies that we have come to believe are hurting people we love. Pastors know they are not only caretakers of tradition or custodians of church culture; they are prophets as well as priests, people ordained by the church to serve God by serving the church. We do not solely serve the church's self-understanding at any given moment. Moments like these remind us that we are never populists who pander to the loudest or to the richest or even to those who are our closest friends. When soulcraft and statecraft meet head on, pastoring is lonely work.

The year 2015 was pivotal for me and for our church. For many years, I had taken the position that sexual orientation was an inscrutable reality for some people but that there was no scriptural warrant for same-sex intimacy. While the biblical passages that seemed to condemn same-sex sexual relationships could be interpreted in ways that showed them to be addressing abusive or idolatrous practices rather than proscribing all same-sex relationship, the Bible was silent on any positive view of same-sex intimacy. Therefore, I repeatedly counseled those who came to me to maintain non-sexual same-sex friendships as part of their duty as Christian disciples. The corollary to this was a "don't ask, don't tell" approach to church life for gay Christians. Since gay Christians could not be married anyway, and only sex within the context of marriage was authorized biblically, all gay Christians were expected to remain both chaste (sexually abstinent) and celibate (single), regardless of whether they perceived themselves to have received the gift of celibacy.

For years, when people came to me to disclose their same-sex attraction, they used words that described their struggle, along with their desire to overcome it. They sought my counsel about why they should be beset with this experience and how they felt powerless to do anything about it. Prayer for deliverance was ineffective. They were stuck, and so was I.

Within the course of one year, five young people who had grown up in our church helped me get unstuck. They each came to me separately and without knowing of the others and shared with me their acceptance of being gay or bisexual. They were not asking me to help them with their "struggle"; they wanted to know how they would be received in the church when they came out. Some asked for my help in their coming out to their parents. Each assumed I would be on their side pastorally, given the fact that I had known them all their lives and they trusted my unconditional love for them. The response of their parents and grandparents in the church was also a shift for me in that these three- and four-generational families were fully accepting of their young people for who they were and as they were. This further solidified my conviction that things were changing in the church about this matter.

Another internal matter of church life required deliberation. For three years, when church members were asked to nominate people to be newly ordained as deacons, the top vote-getter by a wide margin was a partnered gay man. He was a quiet leader whom people saw to possess an exemplary Christian spirit of gentleness and servanthood—the exact qualities we seek in deacons. But knowing that the church had not addressed the role of LGBTQ+ persons in official leadership and being aware that the decision to ordain a gay man would bring attention to the church publicly and have consequences for our relationships to external Baptist entities, I appealed to the deacon nominating committee to pass him over until we could process it more broadly and less personally through congregational discernment. The committee agreed, but after the third year they made it clear to me that the time had come for the church to decide.

Cultural attitudes toward LGBTQ+ persons generally were changing in dramatic ways in the years that culminated with the Supreme Court's Obergefell vs. Hodges decision in June 2015 that enfranchised marriage equality. Suddenly, the opportunity for gay and lesbian Christians to marry and love fully within the covenant of civilly recognized relationships had changed the facts on the ground. Churches were not required to perform same-sex marriages, but they would now have to give an account for why they didn't.

One final and crucial event led me to plunge ahead with creating a process that would lead to a congregational decision. A young gay man who had grown up in the church made a failed attempt to take his own life. When a former staff minister asked him why, he replied that since he was going to hell anyway for being gay, what did it matter? She asked him why he thought that, since he had grown up in a church that didn't teach that. After some discussion, she realized that our attempts to keep the peace by not speaking clearly about it had existential consequences for this man. While we did not say that he was going to hell for being gay, we did not explicitly say he wasn't. He took that for our quiet agreement with the Christian voices that only condemn gay people. I now realized that LGBTQ+ affirmation was a matter of life and death.

Congregations have different ways of making decisions that are not always spelled out in the churches' bylaws. While those decisions most often conclude with a vote of the membership, the path of getting to a recommendation is one of pastoral wisdom. In consultation with the deacon officers, we decided to form a study group that would represent the church in broad ways, but we determined not to ask any of them their view on the subject as a condition of their service. We appointed people whom we believed had sufficient wisdom and openness to be trusted by the congregation. However, no one was included who had made it clear that they had a vested interest in the outcome by virtue of their own representation as an LGBTQ+ person or because of gay or transgender family members. Those people would be heard by the study group, but the group itself was not designed to bring about a desired outcome.

It turns out that despite our best intentions, protests arose about the unfair nature of the process. Some believed that with so consequential an issue, a committee composed of an equal number of people with definite and opposite opinions should have been appointed. This would have ended in a hung jury, so to speak, and left the church in limbo. The hope of doing things the way we did was that it would model an open-mindedness that could lead to changed views under the influence of prayer and study. In the end, few minds were changed: those who began with an instinct toward LGBTQ+ affirmation found biblical, theological, and biological grounds for their view; and those who began with a more traditional view of marriage and sexuality found further justification for their convictions. Few were left in an undefined middle.

The study group developed a comprehensive bibliography. They invited conversations with gay members and their families. They heard from a woman who had been in a lesbian relationship but testified that she had been delivered from what she came to see as sinful behavior and had subsequently married a man with whom she had children. They listened to geneticists and pediatricians. They shared their research with the congregation in informational sessions. They conducted roundtable conversations. Finally, they could not agree on a unanimous recommendation and instead produced both a majority report recommending full

LGBTQ+ inclusion and a minority report recommending that no change take place in the church's approach.

Along the way in the process, I sensed similarities between the way the church had struggled with racial exclusion and the limitations on the roles of women in leadership. Many who opposed LGBTQ+ full inclusion echoed some of the same phrases that were spoken to oppose more inclusive policies on race or women. In fact, I found the minutes of the church conference from the early 1990s when we were debating whether to ordain women. The words were nearly identical, and the spirit behind them was the same.

Some people in the church who opposed the recommendation of full LGBTQ+ inclusion organized opposition to it by gaining signatures in protest. They called themselves "We Love Wilshire," indicating that they were motivated by love for the church as they understood it and had experienced it. They believed that a vote for inclusion would fundamentally alter the character of the church and its relations with historic Baptist organizations. They sent three separate mailings to the church arguing against any change.

The church ultimately voted (by 61% majority) to affirm our existing bylaws that we have one class of membership applying equally to all members. Importantly, the vote was not to change the bylaws, which would have required a supermajority vote. Instead, the vote clarified the meaning of the bylaws without changing anything except application of privileges to all persons equally, regardless of sexual orientation or gender identity.

Specifically, that meant that if straight people could marry in the church, gay people could, too. If gender-conforming people could be ordained to the gospel ministry, gender non-conforming people also could be. Whatever goes for one goes for all, not because LGBTQ+ people are special but precisely because they are the same before God in Christ Jesus as anyone else.

The fallout over the decision was devastating on multiple levels. Friends became opponents, albeit not enemies. Many dependable leaders and givers left the church—in one case a Sunday school class moved together (with a few exceptions who stayed). All told, about 300 members walked out the door in protest. Some claimed they could not abide a decision they believed was a violation of Scripture. Others claimed the real reason they were leaving was that the process was rigged from the start to accomplish the desired end, that a lack of transparency undermined trust in leadership, and that the church was forever changed. They could no longer support what they could not trust. Honest disagreements among Christians are to be expected, but honesty about why we disagree is often hard to acknowledge.

Furthermore, after our inclusion vote, the church was informed by the Baptist General Convention of Texas that it had thereby de facto removed itself from friendly cooperation with the state mission organization. This meant that no seminary students from our church would receive ministerial scholarships from the Convention going forward. It also required that church members who worked for the Convention would have to choose to leave the church or lose their jobs. Similarly, the executive director of the Dallas Baptist Association asked for us to write a letter of resignation in order to avoid being brought up for a vote of disfellowship. We reluctantly agreed to do so.

The devastation of division from other Baptists and the loss of many church members was offset by the joy of new relationships. Within three years of the vote on nondiscrimination toward LGBTQ+ members, more people had joined the church than had left it. Their enthusiasm was contagious and helped many of us work through our grief and loss quicker as a result. They did not replace those who left; nothing or no one could because people are neither exchangeable nor replaceable. But these new members made their own place in our hearts. Gay members testify to how healing it is to be in a church where they are treated as normal human beings who don't have to hide who they are or whom they love. Others came because they want to be part of a church for everybody, but a church for every body, as we like to say. Some of them are healing from the wounds they experienced at churches that required conformity to doctrine or tradition or to leaders who disallowed questions. They are feeling the gentle and cooling breeze of freedom that the Spirit brings to a church after a storm that left behind broken-down walls but also broken hearts.

When I determined that we must face this challenge, it was the product of many changes in the church, in culture, and in me. Jimmy Allen, the late pastor, ethicist, and Baptist statesman, often appealed to the timetable of the Spirit in history. The Spirit of God is patient but persistent, he would say. And when the weight of history's unjust ordering of things becomes too much for God to bear, the Spirit has to stir the church to change, or else the church will die. Contrary to the accusation of many who take this course, I would contend that the church is not conforming to the spirit of the age but to the age of the Spirit.

For me, the decision to address this was deeply personal. Several family members and friends who understood the consequences of this worried about my legacy. They believed I had done my turn and put in my time. It was someone else's duty to take this on after me. But that was like waving fresh meat in the face of a hungry dog: I couldn't *not* do what was before me to do if I believed it was right. I knew that however it turned out, I would have to live with myself every day thereafter.

Having retired from the role of senior pastor in 2022 after thirty-three years, I am proud of the clarity of the congregation's position on LGBTQ+ persons and the resultant unity of spirit and mission we share. It was both the hardest and most rewarding leadership challenge I experienced as a pastor. Pastoral leadership requires wisdom and courage in equal measure. Pastors who lead best stay one step ahead of their congregations—not two steps, or they will lose them; not lockstep with them, or they will lose themselves.

The book of Hebrews calls for courage and perseverance in disciples of Jesus. The Savior's own example is cited: "...who for the sake of the joy that was set before him endured the cross, disregarding its shame..." (Hebrews 12:2, NRSV). The joy is promised ahead for those who are faithful in the time of trial, who are willing to take up their cross in obedience to what they believe is God's call and claim upon them. Sometimes it may mean identifying with those who feel the sting of shame that is placed on them by others, due in no part to the guilt of sin that arises from their own deeds.

Whatever suffering I or others experienced on account of sharing the burdens of our LGBTQ+ siblings is nothing compared to what they have experienced across time at the hands of civil and ecclesiastical authorities. It is a joy unspeakable to reflect on this episode in my pastoral career and to believe that it was indeed all worth it.

The icing on the cake came in January 2023, when our church ordained as a deacon that same young man who had tried to take his own life just eight years earlier. After the service, he sought me out with tears on his cheeks and a smile on his face. "I know this day wouldn't have happened without you. I just want to thank you." And with a hug, he was gone...to love and serve the Lord.

# Chapter 6

# Examine the Fruits

### Rev. Dr. Jeremy Hall

*Rev. Dr. Jeremy Hall resides in Acworth, Georgia, and completed his M.Div and Doctor of Ministry at Mercer University's McAfee School of Theology.*

My journey on LGBTQ+ inclusion is a bit unorthodox in that my head went before my heart: I was intellectually convinced before my heart or my gut knew what to do. When I changed my mind on this topic, I didn't have any close friends who were part of the LGBTQ+ community; a family member had never come out to me; I didn't discover something divergent in my own sexuality or gender identity. What changed my mind was study and education. What changed my mind was the Bible.

I was raised in a Southern, Evangelical household. The Christian school I attended used textbooks from groups like Answers in Genesis and Bob Jones University. From the well-meaning perspective of my upbringing, the "traditionalist" position on LGBTQ+ persons, their relationships, and their place in the church was obviously the only faithful position for a Christian to hold. The six "clobber passages,"[1] which have been used as a blanket condemnation for all same-sex acts, identities, relationships, and expressions, were more than clear enough to my church to establish a doctrine of exclusion. To question the traditionalist teaching on LGBTQ+ folks was to question God himself, and put you at risk of apostasy.

When I finished high school, I attended Samford University (which has recently solidified its LGBTQ+ exclusion policies, severing relations with and campus access to any ministry or group that affirms LGBTQ+ Christians) where I studied religion. I remember writing several papers calling for a softening of rhetoric against the LGBTQ+ community but maintaining a faithful stance that LGBTQ+ folks would need to abandon this chosen sinful lifestyle or, if they could not, live a life of celibacy in order to join the church.

When I started my Master of Divinity studies at Mercer University's McAfee School of Theology, I learned more hermeneutical and biblical study tools, as well as how to study the biblical Hebrew and Koine Greek of the Old and New Testaments, respectively. Once I had the tools to study the Bible in the ancient languages and acquired a greater understanding of how the Bible works, I realized that much of what seemed so clear about the traditionalist reading of the "clobber passages" wasn't actually clear at all. I realized it was an interpretive decision to make these six passages function as a blanket condemnation of the LGBTQ+ community.

Upon this revelation, I was forced back into the Bible to figure out what to do with this new information. What I discovered was that if you didn't come to the Bible with the presupposition that it condemns LGBTQ+ people, then you weren't necessarily going to find it. What I did find were Old Testament teachings about justice and protecting the vulnerable and New Testament teachings on love, equality, and community. At this point my evangelical background kicked in, and my deep love towards, respect for, and high view of the Bible forced me to change my position, because if the Bible says it, I am compelled to take it seriously. I changed my mind not in spite of the text but because of it.

I was furious. I had been pursuing a career as a Baptist pastor since I was fifteen years old, and now it was ruined. How could a Baptist church hire me now? Of course, once I made this change, God brought all sorts of new friends, allies, and brothers and sisters into my life who became my traveling companions on this journey: LGBTQ+ friends and ministers, mentors who were on the same journey, churches that would give me an opportunity to minister and serve in light of my change of heart and mind.

The Bible is not a dictionary. The Bible is not an encyclopedia. The Bible is not a rulebook. The Bible is not an instruction manual. The Protestant Bible is a collection of sixty-six books, with at least thirty-five traditional authors and unknown numbers of editors. It is an anthology of multitudinous genres: history, poetry, biography, apocalypses, songs, wisdom and philosophy, myth, ritual guides, prophecy, politics, and other people's mail. It was written by kings in their palaces, priests in their temple-adjacent homes, homeless prophets, refugees in exile, pastors, and traveling preachers. It was written in three different languages on three continents and by practitioners of two different religions. Amid the epic scale of its diversity, we discover a divine continuity: the dream of God to bless all the families of the Earth. While the Bible can be beautiful in its accessibility, we do great disservice to ourselves, the church, the text, and the world when we act like it is a single, simple book.[2] As Baptists, our tradition has frequently been guilty of this disservice, especially in its Southern Baptist expression.

The perfect case study for this dilemma is the LGBTQ+ community's relationship with the church. For most Evangelical Christians, the discussion is limited to six verses from across the Bible that, in English, seem to directly address "homosexuality" and condemn it as sinful, detestable, and abominable. There is little debate among those who have been taught the method of biblical "proof texting." Why would there be? The six passages are clear.

In Matthew 7, Jesus tells us "every good tree bears good fruit, but a bad tree bears bad fruit. A good tree cannot bear bad fruit, nor can a bad tree bear good fruit" (vv. 17-18, NIV). Yet, when we examine the fruit of this proof-texting theology and the behavior and ethics it produces, the fruit does not look like the Kingdom of God. The fruit of this way of interpreting the Bible has led to broken families, discarded and homeless youth, repressed and lonely adults, sham marriages, drug abuse, child abuse, lives lived in fear, and depressed, anxious, suicidal youth who want nothing to do with the church.

There is a similar story around the church and the role of women. It is no secret that the world that produced the Hebrew Bible and the Christian New Testament was a male-dominated one. The patriarchal system was the primary social structure for the ancient Near East, where women were often treated as property; fathers owned daughters until ownership was transferred to husbands. The Torah contains rules apparently intended to control women's reproductive health and freedom (Lev 11, 12, 15) and guidelines for how women captured as war spoils were to be divided and treated (Deut 20, 21). There are also rules commanding that women be married to their rapists (Deut 22).

Such passages can seem shockingly barbaric. The Calvinist idea of divine condescension/accommodation is useful here; while these biblical laws concerning women as property seem backward, cruel, and morally reprehensible to today's readers, they were progressive in their time and could represent the heart of God pulling people forward towards justice.[3] We encounter similar issues for women in the New Testament as well, particularly in the writings of the Apostle Paul. Paul forbade a woman to have authority over a man (1 Timothy 2:12) and declared that "women should remain silent" (1 Corinthians 14:34, NIV). Scholars and laity alike have argued over and debated whether these teachings are particular to a time and place or if they are for all times, places, and people. The same questions that are raised about the teachings on women also surround the concept of slavery: does this perfectly represent the eternal will of God?

Once again, the Bible provides its own counterpoints through its internal dialogue. The elevation of women comes from Jesus' treatment of them, from Paul's interaction with women like Lydia, from the women who receive the Holy Spirit at baptism, and from the women who are the first at the empty tomb and the first to preach the news of Jesus' resurrection. Prohibiting women in leadership looks increasingly absurd as women around the world gain access to education and ministry training, and men are encountering the unmistakable marks of calling on the lives of female ministers. Today, the LGBTQ+ debate in the church seems to be at a similar point. The prohibitions on LGBTQ+ folks in the church looks just as nonsensical as we encounter the work of God in their lives and consider the Bible with greater intellectual care.

There are three main camps in this fight for LGBTQ+ inclusion: The "Traditionalist" camp sees LGBTQ+ persons as choosing to live in an abhorrent state of open rebellion against God and requires that these persons repent and adopt a cisgendered lifestyle. The "Side-B Affirming" camp accepts LGBTQ+ persons as a reality and welcomes them into full fellowship in the church, rejecting that openly holding an LGBTQ+ identity is innately sinful but requiring celibacy as the only faithful response. The "Side-A Affirming" camp fully embraces LGBTQ+ identities and relationships.[4] For the traditionalists and "Side-B" proponents, the Bible is very clear; these Christians point to the "clobber passages" to make their arguments. Those who hold with "Side-A" affirmations tend to argue that the "clobber passages" are not as clear-cut if you come to these texts without the assumption of what they already say.

A key part of the argument that moved my position (and that would inform my doctoral thesis) is the argument that these "anti-homosexual acts passages," even if they are properly translated in most English Bibles (and I am not convinced of such), do not represent the eternal will of God on the subject of human flourishing, relationships, and sexuality. Rather, I argue that if you follow the grand narrative of the Bible from start to finish, it reveals the dream of God to be justice oriented and community focused. If we read the biblical narrative through a Kingdom lens, we can focus on the perspective and plight of the vulnerable and ask what sort of reading would produce the most love, justice, and liberation for them.[5] I had only recently finished forming this new ethic when I was hired as the Associate Pastor of Faith Formation at Towne View Baptist Church (TVBC) in summer 2018.

TVBC in Kennesaw, Georgia, was commissioned by the Noonday Baptist Association with the support of the Southern Baptist Convention (SBC) under the sponsorship of First Baptist Rome. The founding pastor was well-known and much-loved Georgia Baptist leader Reverend Dr. Monroe Swilley, Jr., for whom the Mercer University Graduate Library is named. The congregation was called into existence to meet an identified need for a Southern Baptist church in Kennesaw as it was on the growing north edge of the Greater Atlanta Metro area.

Part of what makes Towne View Baptist such an important church for this community is its diversity. TVBC matches the diversity of Kennesaw, with an approximately 70 percent white congregation. TVBC speaks multiple languages and has members from multiple nations. The 2021 board of deacons consisted of five women, five people of color, and two members of international origins. This makes TVBC unique among the Baptist churches in its area.

TVBC has also always been something of a maverick congregation among Southern Baptist churches. Despite its Senior Pastor having served as the moderator of the regional Baptist Association and on the executive committee of the statewide conference, TVBC has not always been in good standing with the rest of the denomination. TVBC has been ordaining women deacons and other female ministers for years, allowing women to preach and refusing to adopt the "2000 Baptist Faith and Message." None of these violations of protocol had been enough to provoke denominational action. Yet, in early 2021, the executive committee of the Southern Baptist Convention, meeting in Nashville for the first SBC general assembly since the beginning of the COVID-19 pandemic, voted to "disfellowship" TVBC and one other SBC church for having welcomed LGBTQ+ persons into its membership.[6]

Flash back to spring 2019: a young man visited TVBC. He was new in the area and had worshiped with the congregation for several weeks before the pastors received a brief email from him. The email explained that he had moved to the area to take a new job, and his partner and three adopted sons would be coming to join him in Kennesaw soon. He had been shopping around for a local church for his family. After several bad experiences, he wanted to know, "Will my family be welcome at your church?"

This young father was not the first LGBTQ+ person to visit or regularly attend services at TVBC. The church had experienced an influx of new visitors from the LGBTQ+ community; our church was listed on the website gaychurch.org. This website exists to help LGBTQ+ folks find safe, welcoming, and affirming congregations near them. While it requires that a staff clergy member register the church in the directory, neither the Senior Pastor nor myself had added us to the site. At least one same-sex couple and several LGBTQ+ singles worshiped with us weekly. Most of the congregation welcomed them as participants in the service and even on Wednesday nights for dinner, prayer, and Bible study. But the question of membership had the potential to be an entirely different matter.[7] So the Senior Pastor and I started planning a process. There would be Bible studies, prayer meetings, guest speakers on both sides, real debate, and large and small group discussions. In our plan, everyone would have the chance to speak and listen.

The first step of the process involved a conversation with the deacons, who, besides their role as "an extension of pastoral care," serve as TVBC's membership committee. We explained the situation and our discernment plan. Our membership policy at the time read, "all who profess faith in Christ and have been baptized are welcomed into the membership of TVBC." A few of the deacons left this meeting and went to the senior-most Sunday school class to mobilize the most conservative group in the church. Some decided to stay and engage, while many simply walked out and were never heard from again. This congregational attrition would continue as more of the people with whom we had ministered and worshiped decided that it was easier to leave than to have the conversation.

There were a few attempts to derail the process or have the pastors removed: secret phone campaigns, closed-door invitation-only meetings, and agitators who attended events only to be disruptive. We persisted and managed to host a few of the events that the staff had planned for prayer, Bible study, and discussion, though none of them at the level we had hoped. Just a few weeks after the pastors' first meeting with the diaconate, the church voted. When the day came for the vote to be counted, the absentee votes were almost entirely opposed to inclusion. The in-person votes were unanimously in favor of changing our membership policy to "all who profess faith in Christ and have been baptized are welcome in the membership of TVBC, regardless of sexual orientation or gender identity without exception."

Eventually, when the SBC met in 2021, they had a quick vote. We were officially "disfellowshipped" for "sexual immorality." At this point, the only periodical that carried our story was the student magazine at KSU down the street from the church; now, it was a "David and Goliath" story. The big bad SBC was kicking out a small local church. Everybody wanted a piece of that story. We were soon the subject of news stories and blogs around the country and worldwide, making such appearances in local and Atlanta news as well as in Parisian magazines and the New York Times. With the news coverage came a lot of hate mail but also many letters of encouragement. Some letters even came with financial support: by the end of that first year, over $30,000 had been donated to TVBC. Today, the church's membership consists of approximately 10 percent LGBTQ+ members, and the church continues to teach the Bible and preach Christ.

Upon further reflection, I find that these experiences, while seemingly disheartening at times, have taught me some invaluable lessons along the way. First, LGBTQ+ inclusion is not a gimmick or a growth strategy. There are no half-measures in this decision; partial justice is no justice at all, and as with most justice movements, there will be a heavy cost. Just this past week I read an article showing that one of the main reasons people leave the church is its shameful treatment of LGBTQ+ persons, but reversing course on this important subject will not bring the disenchanted masses streaming into your sanctuary.

At least in the short-term, even if your congregation is ready for the move toward inclusion, you will lose people. LGBTQ+ inclusion isn't a growth strategy; it's a Kingdom issue. As such, it must be done with the Kingdom of God and the teachings of Jesus as its motivation.

There is the potential for great loss over this decision: church membership, friends, supporters, income, job, and even family. The risks are high, but the reward is great. When we welcome the rejected and marginalized into our faith communities, they bring with them immense amounts of pent-up gospel energy. Those who have been rejected by the church without rejecting Jesus in return have so much spiritual intensity in their relationship with Christ and so much to offer the church. When these folks are unleashed on your congregation, you are going to see a spike in passion, outreach, worship, and devotion that can only be called revival. When we do the right thing, the "Kingdom thing," and open the church doors to all people, we will discover that we have allowed Jesus into our congregations as well.

## Notes

[1] Traditionally, six passages from Genesis 19, Leviticus 18 and 20, Romans 1, 1 Corinthians 6, and 1 Timothy have been referred to as "clobber passages" for the harm of condemnation experienced by people who are homosexual.

[2] Jeremy Sean Hall, "Reawakening the Ethical Imagination of the Local Congregation through the Exploration of the Biblical Metanarrative," diss., Mercer University, 2022, https://www.proquest.com/dissertations-theses/reawakening-ethical-imagination-local/docview/2741316617/se-2.

[3] Wilda Gafney, *Womanist Midrash: A Reintroduction to the Women of the Torah and the Throne* (Louisville, KY: Westminster John Knox Press, 2017), 300.

[4] Categories supplies by "LGBTQ+ Theologies 101," https://www.qchristian.org/resources/theology#theologies.

[5] Hall, "Reawakening the Ethical Imagination of the Local Congregation."

[6] Ruth Graham, "Southern Baptists Expel 2 Churches over Sex Abuse and 2 for L.G.B.T.Q. Inclusion," *New York Times*, February 24, 2021, https://www.nytimes.com/2021/02/23/us/southern-baptist-convention-expels-churches.html.

[7] James A. Conrad, *The Rainbow Revival: A Pastor and Church on the Journey towards Inclusion* (Kennesaw, GA: 2022).

# Chapter 7

# Fully Alive

### Rev. Rich Havard

*Rev. Rich Havard is the Senior Program Officer for Wayfarer Foundation and has extensive experience in justice movements and spiritual community leadership.*

In 2014, my best friend from my alma mater, Samford University, started therapy to process his coming out experience. My friend is a type-A, driven, get-things-done kind of person, so he asked his therapist at their first session, "What exactly is our goal here? How will I know when I am done with these sessions?" The therapist chuckled before offering his own question in response: "What do you love about being gay?" My friend, usually prepared with an articulate answer to everything, sat in the serene counseling office dumbfounded. With fresh wounds from his recent coming out, my friend said, "Nothing." The therapist responded to his silence with these gentle yet challenging words: "You'll be done with these sessions when you can answer my question with pride and tell me what you love about being gay."

"What do you love about being gay or queer?" is a tough question for many LGBTQ+ folks. And how wouldn't it be? Most of us have been taught our whole lives to hate our queerness. We grew up with preachers labeling us "abominations." We remember a time not so long ago when nearly every politician on both sides of the aisle opposed marriage equality. I remember being on the playground as a kid when a classmate laughed at me and told me that I "stand like a girl." These kinds of experiences don't exactly lead one to love being gay. Instead, they produce shame, secrecy, and a deep longing to have this part of your identity excised.

So when my friend told me about his therapist's question, it hit me in the gut, and I started asking the same question to myself. In the seven years or so since I came out, I have arrived at many answers through therapy, spiritual practice, deep community, hard work, and, honestly, God-birthed miracles. Today I rarely feel shame; 99 percent of the time, I love being a gay man. I am proud to be a descendant of queer icons like Marsha P. Johnson, Silvia Rivera, Bayard Rustin, and Pauli Murray who paved the way for LGBTQ+ folks to exist and thrive today. I am proud that the LGBTQ+ community is creative, resilient, and powerful. I am proud to be a queer follower of Jesus.

These days, I have a lot of questions about the nature of God, the purpose of scripture, and the future of the church. To be honest, I don't have much interest in arguing about my eternal destination as a gay man, how to interpret Romans 1, or whether LGBTQ+ people should be ordained. I am grateful for others who take up that apologetics work in this book, though, and I know that it is meaningful to many people. As for me, while I am done debating the translation of *arsenokoitai*, I find deep joy in telling others what I love about being gay and how being gay is the best thing that has ever shaped my own spirituality.

Today, I live in one of Chicago's "gayborhoods." I prefer drag brunch to Sunday morning football. At age eleven, I begged my sister to take me to a Britney Spears concert so I could scream-sing "Hit Me Baby One More" until I couldn't speak. Perhaps due to my embodiment of these gay stereotypes, people often have a hard time believing that I also played high school football in rural Mississippi, where Friday nights exist for football games.

I was never very athletic, but what is the best thing that a closeted middle school boy in Gloster, Mississippi, can do to convince people that he's not gay? Join the football team. To be clear, I was not the star player. My father played at the University of Mississippi on a full football scholarship, but the gene pool refused to shower me with his same skills. I was a two-year starter, though, because I worked hard and was a relentless rule follower. I held myself to a pernicious standard. I lifted weights constantly, practiced hard, arrived early, never forgot my equipment, taught my teammates plays, respected coaches, and led team prayers. I knew that I would not be the most talented, but I would strive to be perfect in every other way.

But I was not so perfect in my dreams. Hundreds of times from high school through my mid-twenties, I would wake up dripping sweat, heart pounding, in a state of panic.

I had a similar dream again and again and again. Each time, I would be the goody-two-shoes football player who never broke a rule. In my slumber, however, something would always go wrong, and I would make a bonehead move. I would miss workouts for weeks, disrespect coaches, forget my whole uniform for an away game, arrive hours late to practice, or quit the team. Each time, after years of perfection, the golden boy would mess up and bite the dust. I realize that these mishaps seem a bit trivial now, but to a teenage boy who built his whole identity off pursuing perfection, these experiences were catastrophic.

I would jolt awake, riddled with anxiety. Once I realized that all was well in my real life and that I was no longer a high school football player, I would calm down. Still, this dream infected my sleep for years, and I had no idea why.

In 2015, I told my spiritual director about my dream. She was a gentle, middle-aged woman who loved lighting candles, taking deep breaths, and inviting me to relax. I felt safe and cared for by her, and she created space for me to take off my mask. I think this was the first time that I ever recounted my recurring dream to another person. I had also confided in her that I was gay and scared to death to come out. Skeptical about the power of dreams, I wrote most interpretations off as New Age mumbo jumbo, but my director reminded me that the Christian tradition is also full of powerful dreams in the stories of people like Jacob, Daniel, and Joseph. She invited me to reflect deeply on my dream, to go beneath the surface, to explore what was happening in my soul.

That is when it hit me. This football dream was not about football at all, of course. It was about my life. In football, I planned to succeed by being a perfect rule follower. In other sectors of my life, I designed and enacted a similar plan. In high school, I made straight A's and was the church youth group all-star. In college at Samford, I joined every club and won prestigious awards. In seminary, I polished my resume, got a distinguished fellowship, and honed my preaching skills.

But there was a major problem: in my early twenties, I realized I was gay. This was not part of the plan. Perfect grades and preaching awards would not matter if this truth came out.

In my football dream, I always went from a rule-following golden boy to a bonehead slacker. In my actual life, I was scared to death of going from an emerging faith leader in my denomination, the Cooperative Baptist Fellowship, to a church pariah. From a Mississippi poster boy to an icon of Southern shame. From my family's pride and joy to a stain on the family tree.

No wonder this dream kept disrupting my sleep. My internalized messages about LGBTQ+ folks from my Southern upbringing, corrosive theology, and well-meaning yet misinformed mentors wreaked havoc in my slumber. These messages played like never-ending tapes and infected me with lies: "Coming out as gay will destroy all that you have worked for." "Coming out as gay will wreck the reputation that you have perfected and polished." "Coming out as gay will destroy the vocational calling you have dreamed about since age sixteen." If a dream about messing up my football perfection made me sweat in my sleep, what would "messing up" my curated reputation do to me in real life?

The only way noisy lies lose is when the unvarnished truth drowns them out. I desperately needed the truth, so I tried turning to God. "Freedom, freedom, freedom." I prayed this word relentlessly and emphatically for months, tossing it up to God daily and hoping for a response. Sitting in my three-flat apartment on the North Side of Chicago about seven years ago, in an Ikea desk chair that took too long to put together, I longed for God to move and for "freedom" to shift from a simple word to a powerful experience.

Why freedom? Well, I had lived much of my life in the fetal position—the polar opposite of freedom. Growing up closeted, gay, and Christian in rural Mississippi was no walk in the park. And it gave me potent skills, namely the ability to hide and suppress a key part of my identity, even from myself at times. As I honed and perfected my gifts for hiding and suppressing, I crawled into the fetal position. The football dream was my reality; anxiety, fear, and trepidation were my constant companions.

I had a strong hunch, though, that God had more on offer for me. I believed that God wanted me to live with arms stretched wide, with the wind at my back, with liberation. So I prayed, "Freedom, freedom, freedom." Many days, I would finish my prayer and think, "Well, not much happened there!" But one day, while sitting in that Ikea chair, God moved. On that day in 2015, while I was still a (mostly) closeted gay man, I whispered my freedom refrain, and I suddenly felt my body become physically light, and God said to me in an almost audible voice something like, "Hey, it's going to be ok. I've got you." It is the strangest, most mystical thing that's ever happened to me. It is also the truest thing that has ever happened to me.

At that moment, I felt a surge of power, joy, and verve like never before. The Holy Spirit was pulsing through my body, and I felt alive. I was experiencing new life. The closet had been death-dealing and shaming. It had held me back, suppressed the person God had created me to be, and peddled lies to me about myself and God. But God told me the truth that day. God's truth was catalytic and enabled me to live as my True Self—free and light and liberated. God's truth sparked new life in me and woke me up to new realities. In my dream, pernicious lies that lurked in my subconscious hogged the mic. In prayer, God overwhelmed those lies with the loud and clear truth.

So back to my friend's therapist's question: What do I love about being gay? I love that gay people host better parties, dress more fashionably, and have more fabulous parades than straight folks. I kid (sort of).

Really, though, what do I love about being gay? I love that my coming out experience introduced me to a God who can make my body physically light. I love that my coming out experience forced me to encounter a God who made me accept myself when I could not no matter how hard I tried. I love that my coming out experience helped me tune into God's good truth.

I have more questions than answers about God during this season. Curiosity is more interesting to me than certainty. Stories matter more to me than creeds. But this is one thing I am certain of: God, in some mysterious way, gifted me freedom. The of kind freedom that overwhelms my fears, proclaims the truth that drowns out lies, and enables me to live as my True Self in a way that melts away any mask.

Scripture teaches us that "God didn't give us a spirit of fear, but of power" (2 Timothy 1:7, WEB)[1]. Church father Irenaeus proclaimed, "The glory of God is the human being fully alive." Contemporary mystic and Catholic priest Richard Rohr says, "The discovery of your True Self will feel like a thousand pounds of weight have fallen from your back." I love that my coming out experience taught me how to let go of fear and lean into power. It invited me to live fully. It led me to discover and live as my True Self.

It took me a long time to come out—about twenty-six years—but that experience was the most freeing experience of my life. I feel closer to God, others, and myself than ever before. The ongoing process of coming out hasn't always been easy, though. It has involved gut-wrenching conversations with friends and family, multiple revoked speaking and preaching invitations, being demoted from an emerging young leader in the Cooperative Baptist Fellowship (CBF) to a risky or impossible hire for almost all CBF churches, and many tears. But it has been deeply good in the truest and deepest sense of that word. I would not trade this experience for anything, and I can confidently say I love being gay.

In 2017, the year after I came out, I saw Rev. Matthew Williams, now president of the Interdenominational Theological Center in Atlanta, at a conference. I first met Rev. Williams in 2012 as a deeply closeted and fearful seminary student. For my ordination in 2019, he penned these words, reflecting on his first encounter with me after I came out:

> In 2017, you and I had a conversation in a corner.... it was clear to me that your journey had truly taken you to new ground. Something was different. I saw a light in you and on you that shined in a way I had not seen before. I observed inquisitively and out loud, "Rich, there's something different about you." You quickly replied, "Oh, I came out!" "That's it!" I said. Your weight had been lifted, giving way to a light that had been hidden under a bushel. I could hear in your words an echo of the poet May Sarton, "N*ow I become myself.*"

Rev. Williams had witnessed Sarton's poetic truth that a weight had fallen from my back. He had seen that, through the power of God, I had leaned more into my True Self and had become more fully alive.

These days when Christian colleges like Samford and countless congregations double down on LGBTQ+ exclusion, I do experience anger. I want to fight for inclusion for LGBTQ+ folks hurt by retrograde policies and corrosive theology. But my other primary emotion is sadness. I'm sad, and I say this sincerely, that university leaders, church pastors, and other power players have yet to experience the breadth and length and height and depth of God's love in such a way that releases them from fear, invites them into freedom, and inspires them to believe that "the glory of God is the human being fully alive."

I will keep working for change. I will keep praying for Christian universities and churches, especially queer people who call those places home. Mostly, I will keep living fully because I love being gay, and no one can take away that God-given gift.

## Note

[1] The World English Bible is an update of the American Standard Version of 1901, which is in the Public Domain.

# Chapter 8

# Travelers on a Journey

### Rev. Scott Dickison

*Rev. Scott Dickison serves as Pastor of First Baptist Church of Christ in Macon, Georgia, and is pursuing an MFA in creative writing at Queens University.*

On Sunday, August 27, 2017, our family dedicated our son, MacKaye Benton Dickison, into the only congregation he has known, the First Baptist Church of Christ at the top of Poplar Street in Macon, Georgia.

Our children's minister at the time, Julie Long, introduced him to the church, noting that the inspiration behind his name was the great wilderness advocate and originator of the Appalachian Trail, Benton MacKaye (Benton is also a family name, so that worked out). She said she hoped Mac would come to have that same adventurer's spirit to risk stepping out into the unknown for something he cared about.

She walked him around the sanctuary, as is our tradition, pointing out the stained-glass windows that tell the story of Jesus' life, and told him how his church would do their best to teach him this story. They would teach him about how Jesus lived and whom Jesus loved so that Mac would learn to do the same in his life and help us better learn how to do it in our life together. She told him that God loved him just the way he was and would love him deeply no matter who he grew up to be.

In our liturgy for baby dedications that we said together that morning, as we do for each new child in our midst, we affirmed that Mac was "made in the image of God and is a beloved child of God." His mother and I covenanted to nurture Mac in the faith while his two older brothers hid behind the trees of our legs, and the congregation covenanted to "share in Mac's growth, for he belongs to us as well," so that "he may discover his many gifts and how to use them according to God's dream for his life."

We had family in town for the occasion, and the church provided a wonderful lunch after the service. We ate chicken salad and drank sweet tea.

Later that evening, the congregation would assemble again for a "homemade ice cream social," our annual end-of-summer celebration. We must have brought our Nutella ice cream, like we always do.

It was a wonderful day of church, rich with the blessing and abundance of congregational life. And in between morning worship and our ice cream social, we also had a called church conference to bring to a close our church's process to become, in the words of the motion presented by church leadership, "fully inclusive of all people in the life of the church, regardless of sexual orientation or gender identity."

As I look back on that Sunday that, for different reasons, is special to our family as well as the congregation where I have been privileged to serve as pastor for the past ten years, I am left in awe of the fullness of it all.

The fullness of multigenerational congregational life. Of a child and family being blessed and of a congregation covenanting to help in their care and nurture. Of people naming the ways our lives are intertwined and how we indeed belong to each other.

The fullness of ritual, tradition, and liturgy and the ways these familiar rhythms and words can take on surprising new valence under fresh movements of the Spirit.

The fullness of the gospel and the life and ministry of Jesus, which grounds us in a story of compassion, courage, and grace sufficient to see us through any season.

In one sense, the fullness of that Sunday was simply an accident of calendaring. We did not aim to dedicate Mac on the Sunday of such institutional consequence (in fact, it did add a measure of stress to an already nerve-wracking day—why not add in-laws!).

And yet, in another important sense, it was something more than coincidence that all these things should align, for it was the fullness of who we are as a congregation that shaped and informed our process of inclusion that culminated that Sunday.

## I.

In the late 2000s and coinciding with broader cultural conversations about sexuality and same-sex marriage in particular, many within our congregation began to wonder to what extent LGBTQ+ folk felt welcome in the life of our church. What had the church done to communicate that welcome? What exactly did this welcome include or exclude?

These conversations led the church to take on a study of the issues over four Sunday nights in 2011 under the theme "The Church and Homosexuality." The series was not intended to lead to any particular action or policy change but was an effort to seek better understanding and name questions of concern for the congregation as a whole.

Experts from within the congregation and guest speakers outlined approaches to this issue from scriptural, theological, and even biological lenses. Yet the final evening is the one most folks will still remember, when members of the congregation shared their opposing perspectives rooted in their own personal experiences. Looking back, this seemed to set the tone for future conversations. We would thoughtfully engage the issue from many perspectives, making special room for the personal.

These conversations continued in various Sunday school classes and friend groups and were still fresh in the congregation's mind when I was called as pastor in December 2012. The search committee spoke openly with me about the series held the previous year and acknowledged that it had been an important start to a conversation that would be ongoing, though they did not know just how.

I shared with them that my own transformation toward inclusion and embrace happened in college and divinity school when I was exposed to different perspectives and, more importantly, different people. For the first time, I had openly gay friends and other friends who were struggling to come to terms with their sexuality or, more accurately, negotiating just how safe they felt letting their true selves be known, to me and others. Especially powerful was to hear the ways their churches had failed them by not living up to their stated commitments of love and acceptance. Even more powerful was the witness of those who had held their faith close despite these rejections from their faith community. That struck me, and still does, as a profound courage I have not had reason to discover.

These relationships changed me. They moved me from a place of mere "tolerance" to a place of affirmation and love. To borrow from the Apostle Paul, I am persuaded that there is no greater catalyst for personal transformation than relationship, and personal transformation is the necessary seed for communal and institutional and societal transformation, making relationship the beating heart of any real and lasting change.

As the congregation continued to reflect on what was becoming a more open conversation and on the possibilities the arrival of a new pastor might bring, my first few years at the church were also a time of great change culturally.

Obergefell v. Hodges, the Supreme Court decision that legalized same-sex marriage, came in June 2015, around the time our congregation began a year-long visioning process. These intentional conversations, aimed at giving voice to the best of who we had been and our hopes for who God might be calling us to be, consistently led us to themes of welcome, hospitality, inclusion, and openness.

In January 2016, we took another important step toward inclusion when we ordained our first openly gay deacon. Few individuals were and are more beloved and revered in our congregation than Hunter Godsey. By then around the age of fifty, Hunter had been a member of our church since his family moved to Macon when he was a teenager, when his father, Kirby Godsey, became the president of Mercer University. Hunter had gone on to Southern Seminary, come home to serve as the youth minister at our church in the 1990s, and then been commissioned by our congregation to be a missionary in Latin America. Having recently left ministry, Hunter moved back to Macon and rejoined our church.

Hunter had also reached the point in his life when he was coming to terms with his sexuality as a gay man. He and I had many conversations about what this meant for him and what it might look like to incorporate this part of his life that he had kept private for so many years into his life at the church. He was intentional about this being a part of his candidacy to become a deacon.

Support for Hunter's ordination was enthusiastic but not universal. A few handfuls of folks were deeply disturbed by it and some would end up leaving the church because of it. Others worried that it represented another step toward an inclusion with which they were not yet comfortable.

But the more common reaction on the part of those who might not describe themselves as "affirming" yet was one of sincere reflection. They loved Hunter. They knew Hunter and knew him to be of the utmost character and a person of deep faith. They had seen him grow up, sent him to seminary, embraced him as a pastor, and commissioned him to the mission field.

In the abstract, they may not have been in favor of ordaining a gay person as a deacon. But they weren't being asked to affirm "a gay person." They were being asked to affirm Hunter, and with this the choice was clear.

## II.

Later that spring we concluded our visioning process and adopted a new vision statement that put us on the path to greater inclusion: "The First Baptist Church of Christ at Macon nurtures authentic faith and belonging, loves and serves courageously, and affirms the image of God in all people." We also named a "Hospitality in Our Relationships" task force to lead us in articulating ways we could be more welcoming to groups who do not always feel welcome in churches.

Around the same time, Jody Long, our Minister for Youth and Missions at the time, was asked to perform a same-sex wedding for a child of the church. The couple did not want to have the ceremony at the church in large part to avoid having their special day be at the center of church politics. Again, the church was faced with a question we did not have a ready answer for. In the end, church leadership blessed Jody in performing this ceremony, but it was becoming clearer that we were falling short of the welcome we intended.

Not long after these things, tragedy struck when a gunman opened fire in the Pulse nightclub in Orlando, Florida, targeting it as a gay establishment and ultimately killing forty-nine people—at the time, the largest mass shooting in modern US history. Like so many, I remember being shocked at the brutality and scale of this attack.

I also remember being taken by the witness of LGBTQ+ voices that shined a light on this atrocity. This shooting had struck a nerve and seemed to open the release valve to so much pain. LGBTQ+ voices within the larger church pointed out that for many, gay bars had replaced church as a place of unreserved welcome, community, and acceptance. These places had become sanctuary when church and home were not.

To this point, while I had been open with those who asked about my beliefs concerning the inclusion of LGBTQ+ people in the church, I had not shared those beliefs from the pulpit. In what was to be the final sermon in a series on church ordinances focusing on baptism, I felt convicted that this needed to change.

In a sermon titled "What It Means to Belong," I outlined the history of the wider church's and our congregation's interpretation of baptism and how we are always working together, and we hope with the Holy Spirit, on questions of belonging and inclusion among us. Given the state of our politics and the intense polarization of culture, it may be that offering radical welcome and a robust and meaningful sense of belonging is the greatest witness the church can offer in the present moment. I shared with the congregation, clearly and directly, where I was in these matters and why, and where I hoped we would be.

It proved to be a hinge moment in the life of our church. What had been on the hearts and in the private conversations of many was now out in the open and offered, in humility and with conviction, from the pulpit. There would be no turning back.

In our January Church Council meeting, the Hospitality in Our Relationships task force brought a recommendation that the church council and deacons should take up the question of LGBTQ+ inclusion in our church. They asked them both to consider the ways we were presently welcoming and inclusive and then to consider if further steps should be taken.

This opened up five months of intense and spirited conversation within church leadership. Testimonies were shared. Hopes and fears were lifted. It was healthy and holy and included voices across the spectrum. We debated not just what we hoped the end result would be but also how we should get there. Was a vote necessary? Should we keep these decisions ad hoc as situations arose, or should we take the burden off of those on the outside to force us to make decisions? In the end it was determined that the matter should be put to a vote. So in May of that year, the church council and deacons voted decisively, though not unanimously, to support "the full inclusion of all people into the life of the church, regardless of sexuality or gender identity," clarifying that this included performing same-sex weddings. The same motion would then need to go before the congregation.

### III.

In the following months, a leadership team was named to craft a process by which to open these conversations to the wider church. We hoped to guide the wider church through the same process of conversation and encounter that leadership had taken over the preceding months, but in a shorter amount of time. We did not think it wise or necessary to have an extended process, as this conversation had been alive within the church and the wider culture for the past few years.

In August of that year, the church gathered for three conversations to prepare us for a vote. We rooted these in a beloved hymn of the church that encapsulates, beautifully, the posture we hoped to take: "We Are Travelers on a Journey." Each conversation took its focus from a line within the hymn.

The first, "Fellow Pilgrims on the Road," held over lunch after worship, focused on the role of scripture in this conversation. The congregation was first invited to reflect on what passages from scripture had been most important to them in their own faith journey—not simply in thinking about these questions of inclusion. In small groups around tables, verses from the psalms and the prophets were shared. Parables and proverbs. Stories of the resurrection and the early church. We wrote these things down on large sheets of sticky paper and hung them around the room. In reviewing these things, we noted that the texts typically cited as having to do with sexuality were absent. We said we hoped that in the conversations to come, these verses we had named would remind us of why we read scripture in the first place and would continue to bind us together.

I then led a study on Acts 10–15, when Peter and Paul were transformed through encounters with Gentiles and new movements of the Holy Spirit that directly opposed scripture and tradition of the day, leading them to advocate for non-Jews to be welcomed fully into the life of the church. We wondered together if we, too, were open to a new movement.

We ended the session with an exercise on generous listening. Everyone was invited to take turns around their tables and share where they were coming from in this conversation. The catch was that no one was allowed to interrupt or respond—simply share and listen. We each had traveled a journey thus far, and we wanted each story to be valued in its own right.

We held our second session the following Sunday, this time in the evening. Our leadership team recognized that a part of these conversations that is often missing, perhaps especially within churches, is the perspectives of members of the LGBTQ+ community. This session, titled "Walking the Mile, Bearing the Load," centered the voices of some of our gay members, as well as the parents of the young woman whose wedding Jody had performed months before. We gathered over dessert and heard as one after another these beloved friends and church members offered their testimonies.

It is difficult to describe just how powerful this was. I knew that night, and have reflected many times since, that I have never felt such a movement of the Spirit. It remains among the holiest experiences of my life.

We heard stories of doubt and pain. Stories of inner turmoil balanced by deeply rooted self-love and acceptance. Stories of churches who meant well but fell short, and churches who gave their members the tools to find their own way back to God even after the church itself had left them. We heard testimonies to how our own church, believing that we were "welcoming enough," had nonetheless contributed to one of its own children experiencing such self-loathing and depression as to self-harm and even attempt to end her own life.

We heard of all this, and we heard it from individuals whom we loved and who loved us and the church enough to still be here.

At the end of the session when we invited those gathered to reflect on what they had heard, one of our blessed older saints said to her table, "When we first started, I thought to myself, 'Why are we doing this?' Now I understand."

What until then for many still remained a conversation happening at distance was now much closer.

The final session, titled "Till We've Seen this Journey Through," opened up space for the congregation to share their hopes and fears for the vote before us. We shared these things first around tables and then aloud before the larger group. We wrote them on a large white board in the front, hoping that by naming these things, particularly our fears, we would better be able to hold them together.

We heard from a wider cross-section of the church. Some of our oldest members spoke first, naming in their mind the arc they had witnessed from our open stance in the Civil Rights Movement in the 1960s, to welcoming women into leadership in the 1980s, to now. They rooted what they understood to be this latest movement of the Spirit in the ways the Spirit had moved in our congregation before. Parents of children shared how they hoped this move would help create the type of environment they wanted to raise their children in.

Yet fears were shared, too. Would this result in a loss of members and financial support that would radically alter the church? Even those who supported this move feared the rupture of relationships with people on the opposing side.

In the end, it was clear that whatever the result of next Sunday's vote, we were committed to moving forward with a spirit of unity, respect, and love. The session, which had been opened as an official church conference, was left open until we reconvened in the sanctuary after worship the following Sunday, August 27, 2017, for the vote.

The vote was taken by secret ballot, and the motion carried with 73 percent in favor, 24 percent opposed, and 3 percent abstaining.

After the final tally was announced by the chair of our church council, the congregation joined in singing "We Are Travelers on a Journey," as we had at the close of each session.

Bonnie Chappell, our chair of deacons at the time who served on our leadership team, described those moments after the vote this way:

> The moment was at once triumphant and tender, as the reality of how the church would both change and remain itself set in. The words of the hymn took on new meaning: "When we sing to God in heaven, we shall find such harmony. Born of all we've known together of Christ's love and agony." The church's vote for inclusion and marriage equality rang out in an honest harmony that represented the fullness of the journey to that point. There were a lot of people in that sanctuary, with a lot of different emotions and opinions and stories. But having shared the joys and sorrows of the life of faith, they found that they could keep singing, together.[1]

## IV.

Our son Mac is now six. While he has seen pictures from his dedication and, along with our other boys, witnessed other dedications since, we have not talked to him about the wider story of what was going on in the life of the church that day.

But I know that he knows his church loves him and is blessed by him precisely for who he is and whoever he grows up to be. Just like they love and are blessed by his church friends who have two moms or two dads. Just like they love and are blessed by Mr. Hunter and his husband Mr. Jon, whose wedding photo from our sanctuary sits in a frame in my office, which my boys have asked about and absorbed it without hesitation. Just like they loved and were blessed by JD Granade, our former children's minister, whom we called just a few years after the vote and who became our first openly gay minister. Just like they love and are blessed by all who come to walk with us for a Sunday, for a season, or for the journey of life.

I hope that when we do talk with him and his brothers more about that Sunday and all that led us to it, they are a bit confused before they are proud or grateful or anything else. I hope that they have been so shaped by the boundless love of this church, by the story of Jesus they learn here, by the relationships they find here, and by the fullness of it all that they can imagine no other way to be.

## Note

[1] Bonnie Chappell, "LGBTQ+ Inclusion in the Church," *First Baptist Church of Christ*, https://fbcxmacon.org/travelers-on-a-journey/.

## Chapter 9

# The Blind Leading the Blind

### Rev. Erica Whitaker

*Rev. Erica Whitaker is Associate Director for the Institute for Black Church Studies at Baptist Seminary of Kentucky, a Ph.D. Candidate, and a writer for Baptist News Global.*

She was a sight to behold. Standing more than six feet tall, she was audacious and dark skinned. Her blackness stark against the whiteness of the wooden pulpit. I gazed in wonder at this strong feminine figure proclaiming truth beyond words. At age twenty-three, a quarter of my life gone, I had never seen a woman preach, let alone a black woman. Moderate Baptists complain about Southern Baptists, but Southern fundamentalists don't hold a candle or, for that matter, a burning cross to the independent Baptists who raised my two brothers and me.

We were indoctrinated by the scriptures of King James, Christendom, and the blasphemous, blonde, blue-eyed Jesus. These days I remind myself of the wise words spoken to me by a female Baptist theologian and Seminarian president: "Everyone should grow up conservative. And then get over it."

After a decade of ministering in congregations, I'm still "getting over" the embedded conservative beliefs of white, Western religious doctrine. I have seen how white religion perpetuates archaic dogmas and harmful doctrines concerning gender, sexuality, and race. Please note that I use the term "white" or "whiteness" not in the individual sense but on a communal or systemic level. The system of whiteness is the status quo of our Western, American ideology and religious theology. Whiteness normalizes the attributes, behaviors, and beliefs connected to the meaning and power that whiteness holds. The power of whiteness took hold during the crusades and medieval periods when Christianity became a weapon for the state and a satanic tool of the church used to control the masses. Today, white Christianity continues to use religious and political propaganda to preserve an ideology and idolatrous view of a white, patriarchal God. My journey as a white pastor required new lenses to see beyond my own spiritual blindness. This autobiographical account is my journey as pastor in seeing beyond my obliviousness.

*So what is spiritual blindness?* Spiritual blindness is the inability to see the world as God intended. We can debate until the cows come home about what God intended for the world, but for the sake of clarity, here is a short statement of what I imagine God's intentions to be. *The world God intended is a world where all creation, including humans, live in harmonious communities of love, respect, honesty, and dignity.*

We may not fully agree on this simplistic theological perspective, but we most likely agree that humankind and creation are currently not living or seeing the world as God intended. This brings us back to the issue of spiritual blindness and how we might see beyond our obliviousness.

I believe the solution for spiritual blindness requires Christ-like lenses. These spiritual spectacles readjust our vision of *Imago Dei*, i.e., the image of God in ourselves, others, and the world around us. The difficulty is that we can only find these lenses by being in diverse communities.

As a pastor, I found this to be true in leading and engaging congregations who created space for a variety of different voices including people of color, LGBTQ+ people, immigrants, refugees, elderly, youth, and the differently abled. It was in these diverse communal experiences that I could see God's world through the lens of the body of Christ. I acknowledge that sight is a privilege in our world. Those who are literally blind are considered handicapped, differently abled, and struggle in a world that caters to those who can biologically see. However, I believe that all people experience spiritual blindness. Spiritual blindness is an inability to see both in the physical and metaphysical sense. This can occur during the process of visualization.

The process of visualization involves the eye and the mind working together. The biological sense of sight, i.e., the eye, communicates back and forth with the psychological sense of sight, i.e., the mind. The eye and the mind are in a fluid process of forming and understanding images together.

The external process of seeing occurs when the eye first takes in the image and then sends the information to the mind. The internal process of seeing occurs in reverse when the mind forms the image before the eye sees it. The images that are seen in the mind first are created by a memory—an embodied or embedded experience that is transmitted to the eye, forming the external image. Basically, we see what we want to see. This internal seeing becomes a problem when the images that are embedded from our experience are dehumanizing and distort the image of God in self and others. As a child, the only images of pastors and preachers I saw were also the same images of Jesus—white, heterosexual men. This visualization of who a pastor could be limited my imagination to see how I could be called as a pastor, let alone others who were female, non-white, and non-heterosexual.

## Blind to the Calling of Women

I stared at Dr. Cynthia Hale, a black female preacher and pastor sitting in that chapel service at George W. Truett Theological Seminary, a white male-dominated seminary. Her embodied gospel invoked a calling within me that would take a lifetime to fully see. The vision of my calling might have been blurry then, but by the grace of God I knew without a doubt that I, a young white woman, was called to pastor. Come to think of it, I can't remember a word that powerhouse preacher spoke, but I do recall the first layer of scales falling from my eyes. Like in the biblical story of the curious case of the blind man at Bethsaida, I began to see again.

My healing story of blindness connects with the Gospel of Mark chapter 8. Jesus heals the blind man twice. I envy how it only took a double dose of Son of God's saliva for this man to see clearly. I'm currently on round three of divine healing, and there are days when I'm still shortsighted. Upon first healing, the blind man sees people as trees, which means his blindness came later in life. Perhaps we all are born seeing the world as God intended, but somewhere along the way we lose our sight. It takes a lifetime to see again, and life lessons become lenses to reimagine *Imago Dei* in ourselves and others. The blurry vision the blind man experiences after the first healing creates a conundrum, a communication conflict between his eyes and his mind. His eyes see trees, but his mind sees people.

Whether or not these Tolkien-tree-people images form first in the eye or first in the mind, he is trying to make meaning out of what he sees as well as what he does not see. The not-seeing, aka blindness, is the real issue for the blind man and for my spiritual blindness. Even when I could finally see my calling, I was still blind to the calling of other women. My journey beyond blindness began with seeing the call of other women.

In the early years of my calling to pastor, I began taking on the behaviors and leadership styles I saw growing up. The problem was that the only role models of pastors and preachers were white men. To be quite honest, mimicking a stereotypical white male came easy for me. I'm almost six feet tall and naturally domineering, slightly arrogant, and carry a cool confident charisma. My voice is not terribly high, and I can wear a power suit like a boss. For a long while, dresses, skirts, or really anything that visually displayed an overly feminine presence was cast aside from my closet of pastoral attire.

The Baptist world became the professional playground where my tomboy tendencies helped me rise to a senior pastor position by age twenty-eight. My masculine presence was palatable to the churches who had never had a woman in their pulpit. Both men and women would comment on how they appreciated my lower range of voice, my tall stature, and my direct and at times bullish approach to leadership.

My overly and sometimes forced masculine approach may have helped me climb the food chain of Baptist congregations, but it left me blind to supporting women fully in the church. I remember a dear colleague who identified as a lesbian asking me if I was feminist. Out of my own ignorance I said, "I support women, of course! But I'm not one of those angry feminists." I was oblivious to how I, too, was upholding destructive and dehumanizing patriarchal practices in the church.

Mary McClintock Fulkerson explores this kind of oblivious behavior. In her research, she examines how everyday practices and interactions within a local community are filled with biased behaviors, specifically on issues of race, gender, and ableness. She states that obliviousness is a wound of sorts that limits our ability to see the image of God in the other, a "subconscious or repressed protection of power."[1] Essentially, power blinds. The power I found in my calling to lead as a pastor also created blindness as I tried to maintain the patriarchal power given to me.

In any community where there is a hierarchical structure, there will be an imbalance of power and a strong desire for those in power to maintain their power positions. The power dynamics in Baptist spaces are rooted in patriarchal beliefs and practices that uphold male stereotypes and toxic masculinity as the ideal. This means that even in churches where there are women in leadership roles or even in those with female pastors, the community of faith can still fall victim to patriarchy. It was only after I stepped into my first senior pastor position that I began to change my leadership approach. I had the privilege of working with a confident female associate pastor, pastoral staff who were people of color, and a leadership team with folks who identified as gay, queer, lesbian, and, yes, healthy straight white men. It was during this season that I started fully supporting women and realized that I needed another dose of healing.

## Blind to Color

Let me be transparent. I could only see the preacher who illuminated my calling in the chapel as female. I could not see her blackness. At that time, I was blind to seeing the color of her skin or the implications that her non-whiteness made in that space and in that white community. It would take me years of reflection on that day to see her as black, African American, or an American descendent of slavery. I believed in the concept of color blindness, which was a myth that whitewashed race relations in the 1980s and 1990s. White progressives and liberals started using the term as if the color of people's skin was no longer visible in society and racism was ratified in American culture.

In the five white churches I served, the most challenging conversations on racism happened in the most progressive or liberal congregations. These congregations wanted to focus on sexuality and LGBTQ+ rights and believed they had already worked through issues of racism in their church. The irony is that these congregations not only were predominately white in membership but often practiced tokenism when building relationships with non-white members and non-white communities. The problem is that the power dynamics of racism were never addressed and redeemed in these types of white congregations. This kept all the power of both resources and relationships in white hands. In these churches, the term "color blindness" was often used by those who believed that racism was no longer an issue in the church and in society. Today, a similar term would be "wokeness."

Today, when white Christians claim to be "woke," I cringe. To be woke is to say that as a white person you always see racism or, worse, that you don't see color at all. In my experience, this is an arrogant and impossible vision to claim. As a white Christian, I am hopeful that on the day when I enter the heavenly realms, I will be fully woke. But for now, each day is another degree of waking up to my embedded racism and the explicit racism of the world around me. Each day I get in the arena of racial justice, I wipe away another sleep crusty from my eyes.

The reality for white Christians is that we must keep acknowledging our blind spots on racism and white supremacy. White Christians must keep discovering new lenses by means of diverse theological imagination and non-white interpretations of scripture. For centuries, white Christianity has preserved a distorted theology that Willie Jennings calls a "diseased social imagination."[2] This diseased social imagination is a spiritual myopia passed down from generation to generation. It was almost a decade after that day in chapel when I noticed this genetic disorder in my leadership as a pastor.

The problem with obliviousness is that we often don't acknowledge our own bias or positionality when engaging difficult topics and controversial situations. When blindness in the church goes unchecked, it can create unforeseen damage and power dynamics in the congregation. I find this still to be true in the white Baptist world when leaders in Baptist communities are unaware of their own biases, such as their whiteness or maleness that upholds oppressive patriarchal systems.

Dr. Wilda Gafney, an African American theologian, says, "the truth is that patriarchy is the effect of sexism and misogyny in the scripture, in their translations and in their preaching and liturgical use and it hurts everyone…including men and boys. Exclusive masculine language constructs and reinforces the notion that men are the proper image of God and women are secondary and distant."[3] This is why we, the white Christians, need new lenses to see not only God's intended world but also to see new ways of interpreting scripture together.

## Seeing Beyond Obliviousness: A Biblical Lesson

Scripture can teach us how to see beyond our obliviousness if we are willing to put on new lenses of interpretation. This seeing requires us to reimagine *Imago Dei*, the image of God that created humankind. Now, this interpretation of scripture might feel like a biblical bikini wax. It might rip off a few unwanted heresies.

In the creation narrative of Genesis 1, we find a story of equality, of community, of mutual love, and of human dominion over the earth. Genesis 1:26 says, "Let us make humankind in our image" (NRSV). In Genesis 2, we see the formation and distinction of humankind. The original word for "Adam" refers to humanity as a whole but traditionally has been read as the first male human. Adam has been gendered into the genre of maleness. Gafney says, "Gender Matters. Gender matters in the text, in the world, in the world of the text, and in the world of the translator."[4] But then right out of the dust, we see in chapter 2 a gender dilemma. When the word "Adam" is translated for centuries only one way—as male human—then we get a domino effect of male dominance. When Adam is imagined only as a white, heterosexual male, it creates a patriarchal power system that subjugates anyone who does not represent or is not "seen" as a white, straight man.

This brings us to Eve. We have the earth-creature—Adam and then Eve, the mother of earth. This word does not mean wife, mind you; there is no distinct word in Hebrew for wife or husband. Earth-creature or human is birthed out of the dust, for from dust we all come and to dust we shall all return. Essentially, we are all *Adams*. Then humanity is divided in half to generate diversity. This also means we are all *Eves*. Therefore, the image of God must transcend gender, race, and sexuality.

However, the subjugation of women is caused by a misinterpreted and misrepresented view of Eve in the garden. Many traditional interpretations of Genesis 3 see the once pure and perfect helper turn into an evil witch, biting forbidden fruit, luring the helpless man into an eternity of toil and trouble. The burden of the fall has historically been placed on the backs of women, especially black and brown women.

This brings us to Genesis 16 and the story of Hagar. Hagar is the servant, the slave of Abram and Sarai. I do find it fascinating that Abram and Sarai's oppressive and dehumanizing behavior toward Hagar occurs prior to their name change. The story of Hagar unfolds following God's promise to Abram that he will be the father of a great nation. But when Sarai cannot conceive a child, Hagar is raped by Abraham at Sarai's request. Hagar is then discarded when she becomes pregnant with Ishmael. She flees to the wilderness, where she encounters the God of the oppressed. God then promises her, a slave woman, that she will be the mother of a great nation. Hagar proclaims, "You are the God who sees me," and "I have now seen the One who sees me" (Genesis 16:13, NIV).

In this biblical narrative, Hagar is the first human to see God, to see *Imago Dei*. She sees God seeing her, and then she is able to see herself and see others beyond herself. In womanist theology, Hagar represents African American women. Black women have been at the bottom of the barrel, the base of the Pyramid scheme, and yet in the first book of the Bible God sees the oppressed and the oppressed see God in a way those with power are blind to.

This is simply one biblical interpretation from a black female scholar. There are thousands of new lenses including womanist, LGBTQ+, and other minority groups that help us see scripture, the image of God, and how we can see beyond our own obliviousness. Seeing together requires the body of Christ to be diverse and to embrace difference—different views, different perspectives, different lenses of love. Seeing together calls for the eyes of all, especially those who see the world from the bottom up. It is when we, those with power, learn to see from the bottom up that our eyes will be opened to reimagine a world of justice and equality for all God's children.

## Notes

[1] Mary McClintock Fulkerson, *Places of Redemption: Theology for a Worldly Church* (Oxford: Oxford University Press, 2007), 19.

[2] Willie James Jennings, *The Christian Imagination: Theology and the Origins of Race* (Yale University Press, 2010), 6.

[3] Wilda C. Gafney, *A Women's Lectionary for the Whole Church: Year A* (New York: Church Publishing Incorporated, 2021).

[4] Gafney, *A Women's Lectionary for the Whole Church: Year A*, 24.

# Chapter 10

# Your Story, Our Story, God's Story

### Rev. Dr. Cody J. Sanders

*Rev. Dr. Cody J. Sanders is pastor at Old Cambridge Baptist Church and author of multiple books on LGBTQ+ issues in Christianity.*

My congregation publicly declared their love and affirmation for LGBTQ+ people the year I was born: 1983. Since then, Old Cambridge Baptist Church in Cambridge, Massachusetts, has enjoyed forty years of lesbian and gay pastors. It's a remarkable story for a Baptist congregation (or almost any congregation, for that matter). But that's not the whole story.

Churches don't just come together one day and decide to do something big and faithful and bold out of the blue. There's a story there—a narrative thread leading up to that momentous occasion that is woven from the many strands of stories that have entangled themselves into a rich tapestry through the ages. That living story is what makes possible this next narrative turn toward LGBTQ+ inclusivity and justice.

For my congregation, the more recent part of the story stretches back into their 1960s involvement in the civil rights movement and the practice of reparations paid to Black-led community organizations. The narrative thread runs through the 1970s with the church's involvement in the anti-war movement, serving as a first aid station and sanctuary for people involved in the anti-war riot in Harvard Square in April 1970. The story spins its ways through the converging narratives of the women's and lesbian liberation movements that inspired the women in the church to reimagine faith expressions and work for gender equality, resulting in substantive changes in liturgy and several women becoming ordained and serving in the pulpit through the 1970s and 1980s.

The church's public embrace of LGBTQ+ people started with a gay and lesbian support group in the early 1980s, when the AIDS epidemic was growing and nearly every institution, from families and churches to hospitals and the federal government, turned their backs on the suffering and death of gay men. But LGBTQ+ people weren't the only ones in need of beloved community in that era, and soon the congregation became inspired by other churches and organizations in Tucson and Chicago to join the sanctuary movement. A Salvadoran trade unionist, Estela

Ramirez, who had been arrested and tortured on three occasions for her work came to live in the church's chapel, accompanied by members of the congregation keeping vigil and trained in how to handle a law enforcement raid. Estela later gave a press conference in the Parish Hall to tell her story, and over the next three years she gave interviews to news outlets about the oppressive realities of El Salvador at that time. After a while, her three children joined her in Cambridge and they all eventually successfully filed for political asylum.

These are the large swaths of the congregation's corporate narrative, but the stories of many individuals are woven throughout. And each thread is tethered to the ancient Christian story—an understanding of what the mission and message of Jesus is all about and what it means for us to be called as his disciples. All of these narrative threads of the congregation's story continue to lead us to new faithful work and witness in areas of racial justice, immigration justice, LGBTQ+ justice, and environmental justice. But each new opportunity, each hard decision, each faithful action is part of our longer living story that has brought us to this place, making the questions we face now make perfect sense in light of all that has come before.

Your congregation has its own story, too.

## Telling Your Story

Many churches journey through long processes toward the welcome and affirmation of LGBTQ+ people. The congregation spends years in prayerful study and conversation. Some people in the church leave, unable to make the journey. Other new people arrive, refreshed by the commitments burgeoning in the congregation. And through study and prayer and dialogue and sermons and the leadership of pastors and laypeople alike, the church does something meaningful and difficult and life-giving in declaring the belovedness and belongingness of LGBTQ+ people.

And after *all that good and faithful work* a church undertakes to affirm the lives of LGBTQ+ people and commit themselves to practices of sexuality justice and gender justice, so often *they don't tell anyone about it*. At least not in the ways anyone can easily perceive.

"People know we're a welcoming congregation!" churches say. But with a long history of spiritual violence perpetrated against LGBTQ+ people at the hands of churches, LGBTQ+ people will not simply *assume* your extravagant welcome extends to *us*. We have learned. We have no reason to believe this is the case unless you say it explicitly!

"We don't want to make a big deal about it. If LGBTQ+ people come in the doors, they'll find out we're a place they can belong," churches reason. But we won't come in the doors if we believe harm awaits us on the other side.

We will search out faith communities where the message of our belonging is made explicit before we ever darken the doors.

Once I interviewed a man named Thomas about his experiences as a gay man who left his church in his twenties after a suicide attempt following strong messages of condemnation from his religious communities.[1] Thomas and I were speaking about these experiences nearly thirty years later, as Thomas was approaching his fifties. For the prior three decades, Thomas had been practicing his Christian faith all on his own, without the support of a faith community because, sadly, Thomas didn't know that any faith communities *affirmed* and *embraced* LGBTQ+ people. He had only just discovered this reality, and his excitement about having Christian community again was palpable.

LGBTQ+ people won't know your commitment to our well-being unless you say it clearly and out in the open. So put it on your church sign. Put it on your website (on the front page!). Put it on your bulletins and your business cards and your event flyers. Many LGBTQ+ people long to find churches that take seriously our welcome at the table, but the signs can be so hard to discern.

Too often, we use insider language to describe our LGBTQ+ commitments: "welcoming and affirming" (Baptist), "open and affirming" (UCC), "more light" (Presbyterian), "reconciling" (UMC and Lutheran), etc. But the only people who know what these terms mean are already on the "inside"—those who know the churchy codewords and denominational speak. Passersby on the streets and sidewalks in front of your church who see these terms on your sign likely don't know that they have *anything to do* with the embrace of LGBTQ+ people.

So say it with noticeable symbols (e.g., rainbow and trans flags) and with clearly stated language (e.g., "celebrating LGBTQ+ lives!"). As bearers of the Good News—and the belovedness and belonging of LGBTQ+ people is especially "good news"—we've got to be storytellers of that goodness. We learned that lesson from Jesus! And if the only place we endeavor to tell the Good News story is inside the walls of our churches, there are many who will never experience it.

Last summer, a dozen or so of my congregants attended the annual Youth Pride event in Boston. At this event, LGBTQ+ organizations and vendors set up booths all around the Rose Kennedy Greenway. Unlike larger Pride festivals and parades that can feel overwhelming and replete with corporate sponsorships, Youth Pride has a quaint, community feel, even in a big city like Boston. The entire focus is communicating a message of affirmation for youth all over Massachusetts with community resources and advocacy organizations on display, a dance party, a youth-led parade around downtown, and youth performances. It is so much fun.

Last year, Old Cambridge Baptist Church happened to be the only church that I saw with a table at the resource fair. But there we were, handing out candy and OCBC tote bags for youth to carry around their swag from the other hundred tables. Pretty soon, you could see little blue tote bags dotting the festival everywhere with the OCBC logo and the words "Do Justice, Love Mercy, Walk Humbly" in bright yellow letters on the side. It was a great sight.

Throughout the festival, youth would walk up to the church's table and see our big Baptist banner on the front with a rainbow flag and other signs that read "LGBTQIA Lives are Sacred" and "Trans Lives are Beautiful." They would stand there in front of our table, momentarily stunned. Dozens of youth throughout the day came to the table and said, "Thank you for being here. It's so awesome seeing a church here. It really means a lot."

Twice during the day, conversations grew a bit heavier. Two different mothers approached the table while their teens were elsewhere. Both times, the women were in tears. They came up to me and each independently told me their different but similar stories: They had a child who came out as gay, lesbian, bi, or trans. They loved their child. They embraced their child's news with warmth and affirmation. But they knew their churches would not. So they left.

These mothers didn't leave because their child had been damaged by their faith communities; they left because they knew enough about their churches to know their child *would be* harmed by messages of sin and condemnation against LGBTQ+ people. So they walked away for the sake of their children. It was heartbreaking to hear as these mothers told me their stories.

When they saw our table and realized we were a church that loved LGBTQ+ people, they broke into tears. They had no idea churches like ours existed. They never knew there were churches where they could go with their child by their side and rest assured that they wouldn't hear a message of condemnation placed on the lips of God. They cried because we were there, because they saw our signs of love for their kids, because we showed up and embodied a story of love for their LGBTQ+ children.

Your congregation has a story of Good News to share. Tell it so people can hear.

## Telling *Our* Stories

LGBTQ+ people have stories of practicing Christian faithfulness at the margins of churches for centuries.[2] But largely, churches don't tell our stories—mostly because they don't *know* these stories. LGBTQ+ people have no regular conduit to have these stories passed down to us. In all likelihood, our parents don't know them, our LGBTQ+ friends have never heard them, and unless we endeavor to seek them out where they are published online or in books, we can't imagine they even exist to be found. But the stories of LGBTQ+ faithfulness are full of incredible bravery and love and holy imagination for possibilities beyond the status quo. Our stories must be told, and your congregation can tell them.

Consider the story of the first church founded by lesbian and gay people: In 1946, several gay members of a Catholic parish in Atlanta, Georgia, were denied participation in the Eucharist, as the priest who had heard their confession of homosexuality passed them by at the altar rail. This was not the first time LGBTQ+ Christians were denied access to the Table of Grace, barred from receiving the elements of Communion and the sustenance of community by guardians of the ecclesial status quo. But this time, something audacious occurred that turned an act of exclusion into an extension of extravagant welcome. Renting space in a hotel lounge with a makeshift altar constructed from cocktail tables, a small group of faithful lesbian, gay, and straight people formed a new congregation under the pastoral leadership of George Hyde that took the name the Eucharistic Catholic Church—a reminder of the sacrament once, but never again, denied to them. Let me repeat: this was 1946.[3]

Decades later, another minister with a history of anguished soul searching and, at times, outright despair (a spiritual experience reminiscent of so many saints in the Christian tradition), came to understand his call not to *divorce* his sexuality from his Christian faith but to *vocation* as an openly gay pastor, ministering with gays and lesbians marginalized by their faith communities. Troy Perry, a Pentecostal minister, gathered twelve people in the living room of his Los Angeles home on October 6, 1968, for the first service of worship for what would grow to become the Metropolitan Community Church.[4] The MCC, founded months before the famed Stonewall Riots that sparked so much LGBTQ+ activism, soon became the *largest grassroots movement* in LGBTQ+ history.

While the MCC provided an *alternative* space for worship outside the dictates of the exclusionary churches from which its initial members often came, another group began to work from *within* their tradition to open space for the queer faithful to worship more freely. A group called Dignity emerged as the first effort of queer organizing within any particular tradition: the Roman Catholic Church.[5] Dignity groups met on Saturdays instead of Sundays so that members could continue worshipping in their local parishes while benefiting from the combination of theological discussion, group therapy, and Mass offered at Dignity gatherings.[6] The founder, Father Patrick X. Nidorf, an Augustinian priest and counselor concerned for the well-being of gay Catholics, was eventually barred by his superiors from continuing his ministry with gay Catholics and turned leadership of the organization over to its many lay members.[7]

These are some of the big historical narratives, but there are so many other stories of LGBTQ+ people forming life-giving community, living in audacious faithfulness, and practicing holy imagination. For LGBTQ+ people in your congregation, knowing the stories of our radically faithful LGBTQ+ ancestors can become life-affirming knowledge that we are a part of a history—a queer people of faithfulness—and our history stretches into a future of which we are a part. Tell our stories as a part of the larger narrative of your congregation's striving for LGBTQ+ inclusivity and justice and as part of the larger narrative of God's story in the world.

## Telling God's Story

The time for tepid affirmation is over. Acceptance, inclusion, welcome, and the like are all fine for a time. But now is the time for churches that wish to affirm the lives of LGBTQ+ people and to practice justice alongside us to be clear about why this commitment is important: *God loves LGBTQ+ people. Our lives are sacred. Our bodies are reflections of the divine image.*

And none of these statements are made "regardless" of our sexualities or gender identities but *because those are an integral part of our lives and our bodies.* God loves those parts of us *especially*. Our gender identities and sexualities have everything to do with how we are at home in our bodies, how we experience the world, how we express love and intimacy, how we create family and community, and how we know the Divine.

For too long, LGBTQ+ people have searched the text of scripture to find ourselves somewhere—*anywhere*—other than those seven texts of terror that have been weaponized against us. And for all the good and diligent searching, we only ever needed to look as far as Jesus, *and there we are*. Because the queerest figure in the New Testament is Jesus—at odds with nearly everything around him, inventing and creating and finding places to speak and thrive and live, and *inviting others into the new life of God's kin-dom.*

A story many LGBTQ+ people can relate to is in Mark 6 when Jesus comes to his own hometown and begins to teach in the synagogue—to say what he's come to know about God at work in the world. But his community is incredulous to believe that God could be at work in *his* life; they know him, they know his parents, they know his siblings. Paraphrasing verse 2, they respond, "Where is he getting all of this stuff about the kin-dom of God? Where are these healing deeds coming from?"

And they were offended over him, tripped up by what they witnessed, scandalized. And they rejected him.[8]

His own religious community in his own hometown are the very ones who dismissed him, deemed his life and calling invalid, and became the ones who could not experience the goodness and grace of God flowing through him.

*This was not unbelief in what they saw him doing or heard him teaching.* It was unbelief that God could be at work in the world in ways they had not experienced before and unbelief that the Divine could be incarnate in bodies for which they had no categories of doctrinal understanding, no proper labels or conceptual apparatus of control.

The religious community thought they knew more about Jesus than he knew about himself. (LGBTQ+ people know what that's like.) But in their rejection of him, they missed the presence of God working among them to bring newness of life into the world.

LGBTQ+ folk must keep living our faithful lives of wonder and beauty outside the restricting dictates of the status quo, knowing that when we search the scriptures to find ourselves within the sacred text, we only need to look as far as Jesus—the queerest figure in the entire Bible. We're a part of that sacred story.

And for straight and cisgender people in our congregations, the message in a passage like this is vital: when you know that love and embrace and celebration of LGBTQ+ people is the right thing to do, stop getting bullied by your peers into giving in to letting everybody have their hateful say. Because what you are at risk of missing when you err toward suspicion and scrutiny and offense is not just the wonder and beauty of the LGBTQ+ lives that surround you. You are also liable to miss the very thing you have been looking for: the realm of God come near.

Your congregation has a story of Good News for LGBTQ+ people that continues to unfold. Tell that story so we can hear it. LGBTQ+ people have stories of racial faithfulness and holy imagination that have been lived within and beyond your congregation. Learn our stories and tell them to those who need their lifegiving sustenance. And God has a story of belovedness and belonging for LGBTQ+ people, too: a story of the Divine working in us and through us to bring newness of life into the world. *Don't miss it.* Because then you'll have missed the point of the story altogether.

## Notes

[1] His and other stories form the foundation of the book by Cody J. Sanders, *Christianity, LGBTQ Suicide, and the Souls of Queer Folk* (Lanham, MD: Lexington Books, 2020).

² For this history, see John Boswell, *Christianity, Social Tolerance, and Homosexuality: Gay People in Western Europe from the Beginning of the Christian Era to the Fourteenth Century* (Chicago: University of Chicago Press, 1980).

³ Heather Rachelle White, "Proclaiming Liberation: The Historical Roots of LGBT Religious Organizing, 1946–1976," *Nova Religio: The Journal of Alternative and Emergent Religions* 11, no. 4 (2008): 103–104. For more stories like this, see Heather Rachelle White, *Reforming Sodom: Protestants and the Rise of Gay Rights* (Chapel Hill, NC: The University of North Carolina Press, 2015). I also explore stories like these for their implications for churches in Cody J. Sanders, *Queer Lessons for Churches on the Straight and Narrow: What All Christians Can Learn from LGBTQ Lives* (Macon, GA: FaithLab, 2013).

⁴ Mark D. Jordan, *Recruiting Young Love: How Christians Talk about Homosexuality* (Chicago: University of Chicago Press, 2011), 119.

⁵ Jordan, *Recruiting Young Love*, 113.

⁶ Jordan, *Recruiting Young Love*, 121.

⁷ White, "Proclaiming Liberation," 111.

⁸ Or, as Eugene Boring translates it, "And their encounter with him led to their downfall" (*Mark: A Commentary* [Louisville: Westminster John Knox, 2006], 163).

# Chapter 11

# You Are Welcome, But...

### Rev. Dr. Timothy Peoples

*Rev. Dr. Timothy Peoples holds degrees from Yale and Emory, and is the Senior Pastor at Wilshire Baptist Church in Dallas, Texas.*

Did you watch season four of *Fargo*? It's the story of competing groups who are all shut out of the American capitalist dream. Season four is set in the 1950s, and the Italians and the Blacks exchange sons in an effort to keep the peace. At the exchange ceremony, each boy looks at his own father and says, "Dad, I'm scared," or "I don't want to do it," knowing their lives will forever be different. In a *USA Today* piece highlighting the fourth season, screenwriter Noah Hawley, discusses one of the formative pieces of the season: "I had this idea about these two families, these two criminal organizations, where they trade their youngest sons to keep the peace as an insurance policy. And I thought that was an interesting dynamic. It created a lot of conflict, but it also was a way to look at assimilation and immigration and this collision that took place."[1]

This exchange is fascinating on many levels. However, one thing sticks out—the treatment of the boys in their enemies' homes. The young, light-skinned Italian child lives with the Black family, who takes him in as their own. He sits at the dinner table with the family, prays with them, and even obtains wisdom, advice, and rearing as if he is a "real" son of the boss. However, the Italians want so badly to assimilate into white culture that the inferential question they ask is, "How do the whites treat the Negroes?" I suppose I do not need to go into detail about how they treat the Black child living in their home.

White America, we've given you our children in hopes of peace. But understand what I mean by *given*. In many instances, we have formed them to assimilate into a culture that does not care about their well-being. Through the ages, we have told them to look down and answer when confronted by a white person; to move on when they are called "boy" and ignore when they are called "nigger." Although America poorly integrated the school system, we still got our Black children dressed and prayed for their safety, knowing they were walking into a system that wanted them dead. Our children sit through many history classes knowing that what they are hearing has been white-washed, waiting to come home to read Du Bois, Douglass, Truth, Angelou, Davis, Hurston, and Walker. To know something of their past to ensure a better future. Oh, they smile, yes, they smile because the rule of *Double Consciousness* has been ingrained in them as if it was Newton's Third Law of Motion. Our children climb the charts of success but bear comments like, "It must've been Affirmative Action" or "Someone felt triggered for not having diversity on their staff and hired you, huh?"

They bear the brunt of hearing constant news cycles discussing Black fathers out of the home or the pervasive, so-called "Black on Black" crimes. And yet the Federal Bureau of Justice Statistics reports shows that most crime takes place between members of the same racial or ethnic groups whether White on White or Black on Black.[2] Yet, you never see reporting on the prevalence of White on White crime. White America, we have given you our children, yet peace has not come to be.

I am one of those children. Being one of the only Black families in a predominantly white town, I often remember my treatment as a student. Though we lived in the town because we were Black, we had to get a transfer approved by the school board to attend the local school. One year they did not approve our transfer because parents came to the school board stating, "We cannot have those Blacks doing better than our kids." To catch the bus, we had to run over to the neighbor's house because they refused to pick us up at our home. But the memory that stands out to me the most is a fight my senior year of high school. The school had recently burned down, and our classrooms were trailers. Therefore, to get from one class to the next we had to walk outside in what looked like farmland. On this day a new Black student got into a fight with a white student whose family was prominent in town. As I was walking to class, I heard the Black student yell, "Y'all don't treat Tim this way!" And the white student looked at me and said, "Tim has learned to conform to our ways." I instantly ran to my car and wept. Is that really all I had done my entire life? If I'm honest, I often relive that moment and wonder if I am still conforming today.

My father calls frequently to pray for me—knowing I am no longer home but living out in a white world. In a conversation last year, with tears in my eyes, I said, "Daddy, I'm scared." In his "trying to be strong" voice, he said, "Number 1, what you scared about? Didn't you get out of this racist place? Didn't you fight hard to get multiple degrees? Didn't you go to an Ivy League university? You're in the 'Master's' house, and not as the help, but sitting at the table!" And I said, "That doesn't matter! Just because I have a seat at the table does not mean it always comes with speaking privileges."

You could hear the strength had left his voice. He cleared his throat and said, "They thought we were small and would just die off. We have been waiting for permission from them to be who we are. You can't wait, especially in such a stupid world we are living in now. Doesn't the Bible say something about being more than conquerors?" Trying to lighten the moment I said, "I'm not sure; I should probably read that a little more."

My experience in ministry is different from most. Though I was raised in the Black Church and can do every call and response, I often feel I am just a few white hymns away from getting my "Black card" revoked like Stacey Dash or Ben Carson. I am a big proponent of reconciliation, believing reconciliation cannot happen until we are in each other's spaces and faces. Until we are able to see, hear, and understand the "other." Other than being reconciled to Christ, reconciliation was not a goal of mine. Yet it became part of my calling. For every congregation I have served, I have been their first Black minister. And for a few of these churches, I have been the only minister on staff to come from a low income social status.

Now, just because I believe in reconciliation doesn't mean that every church I have served believes or takes on this action to be reconciled and demand equity. So often the effort comes in the form of lip service. We say we want equity in our ministries until that begins internally by switching out the tune of Beachspring with something that has a beat or a clap to it. We want equity in our worship until the pace of the sermon is changed. We desire so much to be a welcoming congregation of all, but we cannot bear to see our old ways lost.

One of the reasons these seemingly simple things (like our willingness to adjust and expand our worship style and our missional understanding) are actually very powerful is because of the symbolism our worship and mission represents. This symbolism is not just a reflection of our unconscious values in our everyday lives; it also reflects our consciously decided theology. And these symbols have historic roots that span centuries. For example, many Black worship services during early American enslavement were filled with liberation songs, which have been passed down through today. These songs were sung to a rescuing God who freed the Israelites and was being called upon to free those who were enslaved right here in America. The rhythms were meant to physically and spiritually move a person, and they encouraged worship with the whole body. So today, when these spirituals are sometimes sung in white churches, there is almost always someone who comments that they don't "care for that type of worship." But, during the origination of many of these same spirituals, some of the white congregations were singing some of the songs they still sing today to reinforce the hierarchical structure of their world. Becoming attuned to the symbols (including language) of our churches allows us to evaluate and reconsider whether these symbols are perpetuating a conscious and unconscious theology of exclusion.

While I am cognizant that my experience as a heterosexual, cisgender Black male is different from the experience of LGBTQ+ bodies, I do believe intersectionality is required to move from individualistic to communal spaces of equity, affirmation, and change. Not only is our existence tied to another's; so is our ability to see a fuller picture of the kingdom of God on earth. While Kimberlé Crenshaw officially coined the term "intersectionality," Audre Lorde was an early critic of second wave feminism for its lack of integration and inclusion of all people, arguing that feminism should consider the multiple forms of oppression different groups of individuals experienced based on race, gender, sexuality, marital status, religion, and other categories. Lorde's emphasis, in the third wave of feminism, on womanist and mujerista values was essential in explaining the multiple levels of oppression non-white individuals experience. Through her poetry and writings, Lorde was committed to shedding light on the seriousness of intersectionality and how equality and equity are worlds apart. I do not believe it is unfair to say her work called for dismantling systems and methods that were unable to become equitable. As Rachel A. Dudley states, "Audre Lorde, perhaps better than anyone else, articulated an experience of overlapping oppressions and generated scholarship that helped make feminism pay attention to these issues. She was a self-defined Black, lesbian, feminist, mother, and poet warrior who refused to live a single-issue life and therefore called for a multi-issued feminist movement."[3]

I am not suggesting that the church needs to be dismantled, but if the church, of all systems, cannot rectify its role in perpetuating unequitable systems, then we must deconstruct what prevents us from becoming equitable. This includes deconstructing the intersectionality of the ways in which the church interacts with and affirms individuals from every gender, socioeconomic status, race, ethnicity, class, sexuality, religion, disability, weight, and physical appearance. So many people in our world have been hungry for the potential the church has to offer but have been displaced by what the church currently stands for. The church has advertised tolerance but not diversity or equity, sending a resounding message that "you can be with us, but you aren't one of us." The church has pushed people to literally feed on loneliness and say it is holy, good, and right. I journeyed with two churches in their own discovery and revelation of becoming open and affirming. For one of those churches I asked, "Shouldn't this be tied together with the larger intersection of those oppressed by the church?" And the response I received from one minister was, "Haven't African Americans figured it out by now?"

For another church, while there have always been individuals in the LGBTQ+ community, and even some in leadership, a group of people believed this was wrong. Some stated, "The Greek or Hebrew translation does not matter. English is the only translation that has weight because that's what Franklin Graham and Donald Trump use." In some cases, I reminded them that there had been leaders in the church in the past who were gay. I particularly remember one individual replying, "They were all men and wealthy. This person is neither." In my last effort, I shared sermons from past pastors, including the church's "favorite pastor," who believed "all were included in the Kingdom of God, no matter what." A few people took on a spirit of curiosity rather than judgment and desired to study more. The others threw the sermons away and stated that they knew the pastors better and believed the pastors were just saying that for better offerings in the Sunday morning collection. The impact of certain individuals' words was truly damaging, real, and horrific. During my time at that church, I would receive around two calls a month from individuals in the community attempting suicide. For many of these individuals, their contemplation of suicide revolved around their sexuality. I did not need to have the encounters I did with these beloved individuals to know the harmful and damaging effects of a condemning theology, including the refrains of "You're welcome here! *But….*" However, these encounters furthered my calling to preach a gospel of inclusion and intersectional contemplation even if it meant losing my job.

As one who found discrimination from the church and fed on loneliness myself, it is sometimes hard to comprehend what Jesus meant when offering us the chance to "taste and see." But it is harder for me to believe that a God who put on skin to experience the world would ask for us to condemn and exclude while offering loving mercy for all people! And so it is truly hard to believe that the best the church has to offer is a weak, punitive, judgmental, lukewarm, condemning model of community. That is certainly not love at all.

I lean on these words from Julian of Norwich, and I invite you to do the same:

> I was astonished that it managed to survive: it was so small that I thought that it might disintegrate. And in my mind, I heard this answer: "It lives on and will live on forever because God loves it." And so, all things have their beginning by the love of God. In this little thing I saw three properties. The first is that God made it. The second that God loves it. And the third, that God keeps it.[end block quote]

No matter who you are, you have been made, loved, and kept by God. The church's decision to pursue the work to affirm that does not negate or stop this love.

## Notes

[1] G. Levin, "'Fargo' Season 4: Chris Rock on 'playing my grandfather' as a Kansas City mob boss," *USA Today*, September 24, 2020, https://www.usatoday.com/story/entertainment/tv/2020/09/24/fargo-chris-rock-how-crime-boss-role-echoes-own-grandfather/5858654002/.

[2] R. E. Morgan and J. L. Truman, *Criminal Victimization, 2019*, Bureau of Justice Statistics, September 13, 2020, https://bjs.ojp.gov/content/pub/pdf/cv19.pdf.

[3] Rachel. A. Dudley, "Confronting the Concept of Intersectionality: The Legacy of Audre Lorde and Contemporary Feminist Organizations," *McNair Scholars Journal* 10, no. 1 (2006): article 5. Available at https://scholarworks.gvsu.edu/mcnair/vol10/iss1/5.

# Chapter 12

# At Last, Your Truth

### Rev. Junia Joplin

*Rev. Junia Joplin is an Associate Pastor at the Metropolitan Community Church of Toronto and a veteran of Baptist ministry. She preached this sermon on June 14, 2020, at Lorne Park Baptist, where she served as pastor.*

> ¹That day Jesus went out of the house and sat down beside the lake. ²Such large crowds gathered around him that he climbed into a boat and sat down. The whole crowd was standing on the shore. ³He said many things to them in parables: "A farmer went out to scatter seed…. ⁴⁴The kingdom of heaven is like a treasure that somebody hid in a field, which someone else found and covered up. Full of joy, the finder sold everything and bought that field. ⁴⁵Again, the kingdom of heaven is like a merchant in search of fine pearls. ⁴⁶When he found one very precious pearl, he went and sold all that he owned and bought it." (Matthew 13:1-3, 44-46, CEB)[1]

"And at last," wrote the poet Audre Lorde, "you'll know with surpassing certainty that only one thing is more frightening than speaking your truth. And that is not speaking."[2]

*Tell the truth.*

When I took a course in seminary called "The Life and Work of the Pastor," our professor offered us those three simple words as one of the most important rules to guide us as we prepared to enter our sacred vocations.

*Tell the truth.*

What we learned, as we continued to sit under that professor's wisdom, was that when he admonished us to tell the truth, he was *not* letting us in on the secret to smooth sailing through life and ministry. Not at all.

You see, back in the 1960s, when he told the truth to his all-white, Southern Baptist church—when he told them he thought it was wrong that their bylaws made it so Black people could not become church members, and when he told them he was going to work to change those bylaws—he got himself into a fight that consumed ten years of his ministry career.

Ask the prophets what happens when you tell the truth. Jeremiah will tell you about it from that well they tossed him into. Ask women what happens when they tell the truth about harassment and assault, often to find they've only become the targets of more harassment and assault.

I guess telling the truth is easier said than done. Maybe truth-telling isn't valued as highly as we like to think. Maybe my teacher understood that. Maybe that's why he was so determined to imprint those words upon us.

Tell. The. Truth.

When you live much of your life in the pulpit, you are constantly dealing with temptation to sidestep or gloss over or make compromises with the truth. You've seen and heard about how it can go wrong, so you develop a preference for "truthiness" instead of truth. Stephen Colbert coined that word about fifteen years ago. Truthiness—that which seems true without actually having to be true. That which reflects what we, in our biases, *want* to be true. Sometimes, it's easier to be truthy in the pulpit than it is to be *truthful*.

The justifications for this are many:
*You've got to pick your battles.*
*I just don't think my people are ready for that.*
*Change comes slowly.*
*If you say it that way, you're gonna lose people.*
*Nobody's going to listen to that.*
*Nobody wants to hear that stuff.*
*That's too controversial; it's too political.*
*People come to church to feel good.*
*It's not worth the trouble. It's too risky.*

The Brazilian priest and liberation theologian Dom Hélder Câmara once said, "When I give food to the poor, they call me a saint. When I ask *why* they are poor, they call me a communist."[3] That's the kind of thing you say when you've learned how costly speaking the truth can be.

I'm afraid that a great many of us preachers—and a great many of us believers—would rather hand out food than confront challenging truths about hunger and poverty. Or, as we're discovering in this tumultuous season, we would rather take comfort in our insistence that all lives matter than confront the hard truths being told when people proclaim that Black Lives Matter.

*Tell the truth.*

Recognize, however, that it comes with a cost.

Jesus, in his wisdom, once said that the Kingdom of Heaven, like the truth, is costly. God's great dream for the world, Jesus said, is like a treasure hidden in a field. Or it's like a pearl so valuable, it can put a spark in the eye of even the most seasoned pearl collector.

It's out there to be found. It's beautiful, but it'll cost you.

Jesus loved to tell those kinds of stories. They were his trademark. I read from Matthew 13 this morning, and that chapter goes on and on, listing one story after another, with a few verses of interpretation tossed into the mix. But more often it's the case that these stories—these *parables*—don't include any kind of explanation. Instead, they invite us along our *own* journeys of interpretation. They are like sacred setups, and Jesus is often counting on his hearers to start making their own connections and thinking about their own punch lines.

With that in mind, sometimes I wonder about the two treasure seekers in the parables I read today. Something in their decision-making seems rash…foolish, even. After all, these are two stories about people liquidating *all* their assets, selling off *all* they owned. How did that even work? How long did it take? And how could it have possibly happened quickly enough that they didn't stop to think, *Wait… am I sure about this?*

*This is a rare and precious treasure, for sure. But is it precious enough to justify selling off everything else? A field with a treasure in it is lovely, I guess. But what am I going to eat? Where am I going to sleep?*

*This is an exquisite pearl, no question about it. But is it really worth selling all my stuff and emptying my bank account? At least the other guy got a field. You can't build a house or grow food in the middle of a pearl.*

These people seem like they're making such crazy decisions. And yet…

For some reason, Jesus wants us to know that this seemingly indefensible risk is actually a fitting example of what God dreams about when God imagines what creation could be. That's what the Kingdom, the family, the beloved community of God is like.

Because sometimes, God calls us in the direction of something that is so beautiful and so precious, something that enkindles such abundant and undeniable joy, well, you've just gotta point yourself in that direction and go.

It's my belief that we are all treasure seekers in some way or another. Seeking something that is precious, something that is beautiful and true. But I'm not so sure our stories look like the ones we've heard from Matthew 13 today. I don't think there are many of us who would grasp at treasure with such wanton abandon—no matter how much joy it might promise us.

My suspicion is, if *we* were living out either of those parables, our conditioning would kick in and we'd manage to talk ourselves out of it.

We would remember how much safer it is to settle for truthiness instead of truth…how often we've seen the world make an example out of the risk takers. The dreamers. The prophets. The poets. The rebels. The pastors, too—and probably a number of other people you know.

So my suspicion is, we would let that treasure go.

We'd let that treasure go, and maybe we'd give it a passing thought now and then. Perhaps we'd lament our missed chance a moment or two before the cynicism within us spoke up and said "It wasn't really worth it" or "It would have never worked, you know." We'd believe that voice. And we might even convince ourselves to put those thoughts out of our minds entirely. To busy ourselves with other pursuits, lesser pursuits.

It's sad, isn't it, to think about those missed chances. About all the treasures left buried in unpurchased fields. All the precious pearls left unsold. It would be very sad, indeed, if that's how the stories ended.

But God is love, friends. Our scriptures tell us so. And our scriptures tell us also that love never ends. And there's our good news—because our Source of Endless Love will never be content with stories ending that way. With treasures undiscovered. With precious pearls unsold. Jesus reminds us, in some of his other stories, that God is relentless about such pursuits.

So maybe that pearl has to sit in the case in the jewelry store for a while. Maybe the dream has to go undreamed, or the truth ends up not being spoken for a while.

Just know that God, the wildest dreamer and most persistent treasure seeker of them all, isn't One to give up. God is the One who makes a way where there is no way. God is the One who knows you more fully than you know yourself, the One who knit you together in your inmost being. God is the One who made you, fearfully and wonderfully.

God has a way of guiding you, by the same fear and wonder, to the place where you'll find your treasure. To the shop where your pearl just happens to be for sale. To the moment when you can't do anything else but speak your big, risky truth, no matter how much trouble it gets you into.

I stepped into the pulpit for the first time when I was eleven years old. I had been listening to what I was certain was the voice of God. I heard that voice calling me to be a pastor. And that's what I did. I have been following that calling—and finding my way into one pulpit or another—for thirty years. I *thought* that was my treasure.

And it was. Sort of. But there was more. Maybe I didn't realize it at the time, but there was more. God had more to say to me back then than "You're supposed to be a pastor."

The fullness of my treasure, the wholeness of my truth, wasn't entirely clear in those days. So, in much the same way that we settle for truthiness instead of truth, I settled for half a treasure. A pearl that was nice enough, but not the kind of precious that sets God dreaming.

Ultimately, graciously, we are led by the Divine Treasure Seeker to that place where "at last [we] know with surpassing certainty that only one thing is more frightening than speaking [our] truth. And that is not speaking."

Even if the cost seems too high. Even if the consequences seem too great. Even if the landing seems too hard and the leap of faith God wants you to make feels like madness.

God isn't going to stop calling us. God isn't going to let up until we've arrived at the point where we accept that it's time to cash out our accounts and say, "Alright. Let's buy that pearl."

I've been thinking about that point for a very long time. It is a point I suspected I had let pass me by. But God is gracious, and God makes a way. And friends, with the divine joy of one finally getting her hands on a most precious pearl, I want you to hear me when I tell you I'm not just supposed to be a pastor; *I'm supposed to be a woman.*

Hi, friends. Hi, family.

My name is Junia.

You can call me June.

I am a transgender woman, and my pronouns are she and her.

That's the treasure, folks. That's the truth I can't help but speak. Until now, I didn't know *how* or *when* or *whether* to speak. I thought it was impossible. I thought it was sinful. I thought it was too costly. But I have learned; and I have grown; and I have discovered that the only thing that costs more than buying the treasure God creates us to find is *not* buying it.

In sharing this truth with you today, I'm saying that I want to be the person God created me to be, that I want to experience the health and wholeness and the abundance of life Christ has been calling me to experience since the time when I first believed and followed.

I realize, of course, that I may be taking an enormous risk here; that possessing this pearl may truly cost me everything. It's scary, but I read someplace that love casts out fear.

So if you're listening to this message and you're part of the Lorne Park Baptist family, another truth I want you to hear me say is, *I love you and I still love being your pastor.* I hope that we can find ways as a family of faith to walk together in that love. I hope we can model grace and compassion in a way that very few churches have ever done. I hope we can demonstrate courage and vulnerability and listen together as God calls us to imagine what a vibrant, life-affirming ministry can look like here at the beginning of our second hundred years.

I had hoped to share this truth with you in person. The onset of COVID-19 closed that door, but perhaps another door has opened. We are living in a world where we're asking important questions about what really matters; we're also making broader connections than we ever have before.

So maybe you're receiving this message and you're someplace else. Geographically. Religiously. Theologically. Socially.

Maybe you can give some thought to what you're seeing and what you're hearing. Maybe you're part of another faith community, and you're wondering what this might look like at your church. Regardless of how you're connected to me, I hope that, by answering God's call and speaking my truth, I'll inspire you to do the same.

Finally, to my LGBTQ+ siblings in my family of faith and beyond…and to the millions of you who are or were people of faith: I see you. You are not alone. As an ordained minister of the gospel, as someone on whom the church has laid hands and said "You can speak for us," I want you to hear me say that you are fearfully and wonderfully made. Beautifully made in God's image. A perfect reflection of God's matchless creativity. No matter your orientation or gender. And I want you to hear me say that God delights in you and feels pure joy for you for having discovered your treasured identity.

I am sorry for the times you have been lied to about who you are in the eyes of God. I am sorry for the times you have been told that who you are is sinful or broken, whether it's some raving fundamentalist in a suit and tie or his kinder, gentler counterpart in jeans and sneakers at the hip church in the movie theater. It's not true. Those words are deceitful and evil, and we have already lost too many siblings to that deadly theology.

In particular, I want to proclaim to my transgender siblings that I believe in a God who knows your name, even if that name hasn't been chosen yet. I believe in a God who calls you a beloved daughter even if your parents insist you'll always be their son. A God who blesses you and gives you a home even if you're not welcome in the place you used to call home. A God whose relentless creativity invites you to become who you were created to be, even if you have to risk everything to do it.

That's the call that comes to every one of us. Regardless of our gender or orientation or age or ethnicity or status.

You are loved. Loved with an everlasting love.

That Love frees you to find your pearl…to become the person you were meant to be.

And I don't know what that ministry is going to look like, exactly. But by the goodness and grace of Jesus, I am going to speak that truth…I'm going to share this abundant treasure…and I am going to proclaim that good news for as long as I have breath.

Hallelujah.

Praise and thanks be to the Lord, the Holy One, the Creator, the risker of risks, and the seeker of precious treasures.

Amen.

## Notes

[1] Scripture quotations from the COMMON ENGLISH BIBLE. © Copyright 2011 COMMON ENGLISH BIBLE. All rights reserved. Used by permission. (www.CommonEnglishBible.com).

[2] Audre Lorde, *Sister Outsider: Essays and Speeches* (Berkeley, CA: The Crossing Press, 1984), 45.

[3] S. Claibourne and J. Wilson-Hartgrove, *Common Prayer: A Liturgy for Ordinary Radicals* (Grand Rapids, MI: Zondervan, 2010), 450.

# Chapter 13

# How Homophobia Leads to Universalism

### Rev. Dr. Brett Younger

*Rev. Dr. Brett Younger is the Senior Minister at Plymouth Church in Brooklyn, New York.*

The first Bible rolled off Gutenberg's press with less discussion than the 2008 Broadway Baptist Church, Fort Worth directory. We began the process thinking, "What's more fun than a church directory? What's not delightful about eight-year-old boys wearing ties that make them look less like themselves than anyone else? What could possibly go wrong?"

I imagined signing directories like high school annuals: "You made class wacky." "Always be yourself. Unless you can be a unicorn, then definitely be a unicorn." "U r 2 sweet 2 b 4 got 10."

## Who's in Your Church Directory?

If you were at Broadway Baptist and paying attention, you were not surprised when a male couple who had been with each other for twelve years had their picture made together. Broadway Baptist had gay members for decades. Van Cliburn, the great classical pianist, joined in the 1960s and was involved in a very public palimony suit in the 1990s. He gave the church grand pianos that no one wanted to give back.

The church directory committee had no clue there was an issue until one person alerted her Sunday school class that it was time to go to war. This was a chance for the old conservative guard to take back their church after what they saw as a thirty-year slide to the left. They argued that same-sex couples could not be pictured together in their church directory because it would not depict the "biblical view of the family." Some on the conservative side were photographed with their pets. Does that raise questions?

The staff naively thought this could be an opportunity for growth and understanding. Two New Testament professors from Southwestern Seminary and Brite Divinity School came to debate the issue. They ended up not liking one another at all.

Tony and Peggy Campolo argued in front of us. At the time, she was to the left, and he was to the right. (Tony has since called for the full acceptance of gay people.) They were honest about the absurdity of condemning anyone for an orientation with which they were born.

Most of the people who were against including gay people in the church avoided talking to gay people in the church. The same-sex couples, who were mistreated by individuals in the congregation, stayed because of their love for Christ.

We talked about the peculiar verses that were never the point. Genesis 19 is about a gang rape in Sodom and Gomorrah. Jesus says the sin was a lack of hospitality (Luke 10:11-12). Leviticus 18:22 and 20:13 are about using sex for power. (The Levitical laws include prohibitions against eating shrimp, growing two crops in the same field, wearing polyester, picking up sticks on the Sabbath, and naming your genitals. These laws do not concern most church people.)

Romans 1:26-27 is about pedophilia and promiscuous sex in the temple. In 1 Corinthians 6:9-10 and 1 Timothy 1:9-10, Paul avoids first-century words for gay sex, instead creating a word to describe religious sex rituals and exploitative sex-for-sale. Neither Paul nor the writers of the Hebrew scriptures use words that describe a committed same-sex relationship. Using the words for pedophilia and homosexual promiscuity against committed gay couples is not fair. Those against gay people in the church used a few strange verses as a way of protecting a tired old prejudice. Those who wanted to include everyone had the story of Jesus and the central message of the gospel, but as long as there is heterosexual privilege, there will be homophobia.

When leaders of the Southern Baptist Convention, the Baptist General Convention of Texas, and the Fort Worth Baptist Association found out that we were talking about what scripture actually said, they let us know that if we pictured gay couples in our directory, we would be kicked out of their organizations. Angry people made a point of sharing their angry views with me. Sinful people wanted to explain their definition of a sinful lifestyle.

They offered me $50,000 to resign and threatened me with a bylaws provision. If 100 people signed a petition, the church had to vote on that issue, and so they prepared a petition to fire me.

The deacon chair suggested I make the bribe public. This surprised the people who were upset with the direction of the church. They expected me to leave without a vote. One deacon said, "I've fired two pastors. I can fire this one."

After ten different pieces of bulk mail were mailed to every member, and front-page stories appeared in *The Dallas Morning News* and *Fort Worth Star-Telegram*, the church voted to keep the pastor 499–237.

## The Same Tired Argument

Many of the angriest people left the church because they had seen this moment as their last stand. Someone at the McAfee School of Theology read the news and invited me to come and teach. I told myself I took this new job because I could not be a good minister for those who wanted me to leave, but I was also tired of an old argument.

Fifteen years later, I have decided that this is what I should have been saying from the start: The argument over the inclusion of gay Christians is just another version of a tired old wrong-headed debate.

Most church fights can be summed up by Rudyard Kipling's "We and They":

> All good people agree,
> and all good people say,
> all nice people, like Us, are We
> and everyone else is They.
> But if you cross over the sea,
> instead of over the way,
> you may end by (think of it!) looking on We
> as only a sort of They!

## The Same Tired Argument: Aporophobia

Before we had the great directory debate, Broadway Baptist had the same tired argument about the inclusion of poor people. The Missions Committee wanted the church to participate in Room in the Inn, a program in which homeless people spend the coldest nights of the year in the church building. The church had two clothing rooms, a food pantry, meals for the homeless, an after-school program, and a history of making sure there were lines between the rich and the poor.

Almost without exception, the people who didn't want gay people in the building didn't want poor people in the building either. We had eight churchwide meetings before 66 percent of the church voted not to let people freeze to death on the sidewalk. The arguments over including the poor and including same-sex couples were painfully similar. Many argued that *they* were not *us* and that the church belonged to *us*.

We keep repeating this centuries-old argument. We have different churches for the rich, the poor, Democrats, Republicans, white people, black people, gay people, heterosexual people, churches with Starbucks in the lobby, and churches where the coffee only comes in one flavor. We have created practices, policies, and peculiar biblical justifications to keep out people who are not like us. We have repeated the same tired argument.

## The Same Tired Argument: Sectarianism

In 1973, my church's youth minister warned us about "mixed dating." Tommy said, "I want to tell you about an error in judgment I made because I don't want you to make the same mistake. I saw her on the first day of senior English. I was in love, but I didn't ask Donna out on a date until October. We went to see *The Jungle Book*, but I wasn't paying attention to the message—that the jungle boy needed to be with his own kind. Like Mowgli, Donna and I didn't talk about the elephant in the room. For six months, we did everything together, except for the most important thing. We didn't go to the same church. You see, Donna was a Methodist, so we ended up with broken hearts. Amos 3:3 and 2 Corinthians 6:14 warn us about being unequally yoked. Don't date someone you can't marry."

Tommy had selected Bible verses, church traditions, and walls that he thought mattered. Tommy had a tired old argument, but as long as groups want to feel superior, there will be sectarianism.

## The Same Tired Argument: Racism

In 1974, my father was the pastor of Calvary Baptist Church in West Point, Mississippi. Melanie, a seventh grader, invited her best friend Carlene, an African American, to our church gym for our youth revival. Melanie and Carlene made their way to folding chairs near the midcourt. The ushers gathered to decide how to deal with this thirteen-year-old threat to their Christianity. Wayne, a Little League baseball coach, asked Carlene to leave. Melanie went with her. The next night, two members of the Klan and the deacon board were stationed at the door to make sure no African Americans tried to worship God. They did not wear hoods—which would have been more honest.

The racists had selected Bible verses, church traditions, and walls that had been standing for centuries. They had a tired old argument, but as long as there is white privilege, there will be racism.

## The Same Tired Argument: Anti-Semitism

In 2019, the shooter at the synagogue in Poway, California, was a member of an Orthodox Presbyterian Church. Rabbi Lippe invited me to go on a radio show with him to talk about Christianity and anti-Semitic violence. I started looking more carefully at our history. Martin Luther, who may be the most important figure in the last five hundred years of Christian history, was anti-Semitic. In *The Jews and Their Lies*, he wrote, "We are at fault in not slaying them." Historians like to say that Luther was great except for his anti-Semitism—which is embarrassing for historians. You cannot be great and anti-Semitic.

Most churches in America today do not think they are anti-Semitic but allow small attacks that make larger attacks more likely. The names "Old Testament" and "New Testament" are unfair. Some Christian preachers suggest the Old Testament God is angry while the New Testament God is merciful. This is not true to Judaism or Christianity. Jesus is often set in opposition to first-century Judaism as though Jesus was the only one who valued women or worked for the oppressed. Jesus learned to value women and care for the poor from his Jewish context.

The anti-Semites have selected Bible verses, church traditions, and walls that have been standing for centuries. They have the same tired argument, but as long as Christians put down Judaism to make Christians feel good, there will be anti-Semitism.

In my experience, the people who don't care for gay people tend to be many of the same people who are sectarian, racist, and anti-Semitic. There must be many for whom this is not true, but they are not the people I have encountered. My experiences led me to a conclusion I wish I had come to decades earlier. We should stop having these foolish arguments and let everyone in.

## The Case for Letting Everyone In

Cartoons picture Simon Peter sitting at the pearly gates looking up names in the book of life. Some believe that one day someone wearing a halo will say something like, "You were born in the right country to good parents, so you went to a church that believes the right things. You are not in any of the unapproved categories. Thank God you're not gay, Jewish, or Muslim. Congratulations!"

However the mystery that comes after death works, it does not work like that. If there is a book of life, the only thing written in it is our names. Our hope is not that we will be pure enough. Our hope is God's love. The argument is old, but the promise of grace is, too.

The Hebrew people were shocked when they heard prophets say that God's grace extends farther than they had imagined. Isaiah writes about a parade of people going home, about God's grace reaching more than just those who have heard God's name: "Look, some shall come from far away, some from the north and from the west, and some from the land of Syene" (Isaiah 49:12). (Scripture references are from the NRSV.)

We can find biblical support for just about anything, but there is a lot of support for universalism:

- The crooked shall be made straight, and the rough ways made smooth, and all flesh shall see the salvation of God. (Luke 3:5-6)
- I, when I am lifted up from the earth, will draw all people to myself. (John 12:32)
- I do not judge anyone who hears my words and does not keep them, for I came not to judge the world but to save the world. (John 12:47)
- Therefore just as one man's trespass led to condemnation for all, so one man's act of righteousness leads to justification and life for all. (Romans 5:18)
- For God has imprisoned all in disobedience so that he may be merciful to all. (Romans 11:32)
- For as all die in Adam, so all will be made alive in Christ. (1 Corinthians 15:22)
- For there is one God; there is also one mediator between God and humankind, Christ Jesus, himself human, who gave himself a ransom for all. (1 Timothy 2:5-6)
- For to this end we toil and suffer reproach, because we have our hope set on the living God, who is the Savior of all people, especially of those who believe. (1 Timothy 4:10)
- For the grace of God has appeared, bringing salvation to all. (Titus 2:11)
- The Lord is not slow about his promise, as some think of slowness, but is patient with you, not wanting any to perish but all to come to repentance. (2 Peter 3:9)
- He is the atoning sacrifice for our sins, and not for ours only but also for the sins of the whole world. (1 John 2:2)

There are so many verses like these. Is that just a fluke, or did these people really mean what they wrote?

The verses on hell are not as strong as I was taught to believe. Hell in the original Hebrew and Greek was "the grave," "the pit," and "the trash heap," but the Bible does not teach eternal punishment in the way conservative Christian churches teach it. Our modern ideas of hell have their origins in John Milton's *Paradise Lost* and Dante's *Inferno*.

Did we ever really believe that God would punish someone forever because of mistakes or misunderstandings? Did we believe that people were destined for hell because of the circumstances of their birth? Why would a loving and forgiving God create a hell in which to torture people?

Getting rid of hell seems obvious to many Christians, but we have not acted on the obvious truth that our churches need to reflect God's love for all people.

## Tearing Down the Fences

I used to tell this story during ordination services. Years ago, a little Roman Catholic village in Eastern Europe needed a midwife, but they didn't have much money. The only woman willing to take the position for the meager salary they could offer was Jewish. After some debate, they gave her the job. She spent the rest of her life becoming part of the community. She was with them in fear, sorrow, and joy. When she died, she left those whom she had loved in a quandary. They wanted to bury her in the church cemetery, but she was not Roman Catholic. The priest agreed to call the bishop and ask for an exception to be made. The bishop's initial response was unequivocal. The Jewish woman couldn't be buried in the Roman Catholic cemetery.

The priest pleaded, "She's family. She brought our children into the world. She loved our congregation."

The bishop finally offered a compromise: "She can't be buried in the cemetery, but you can bury her just outside the fence."

That's what they did. After the graveside service, several members of the congregation went to the pub and began to tell stories about the woman.

"She came in the middle of a terrible snowstorm to deliver our son. It was snowing again when she delivered our granddaughter."

"She was there when my sister had a miscarriage. She cried right along with the rest of us."

They talked about how she helped them welcome life and how she grieved with them in the shadow of death. They were slowly overwhelmed by embarrassment at what they had done. They had buried a family member on the wrong side of the fence. They went to their homes and got their tools. They gathered again at the cemetery and began the hard work of moving the fence. The next morning the grave hadn't moved, but now it was inside the fence, where it belonged.

When I told this story, I used to close by saying, "The church needs people who will enlarge the fence."

I was wrong. I should not have encouraged anyone to be part of the tired arguments over where the fence should be. I used to applaud the people who moved the fence, but I can't do it anymore. We need to destroy the fence. We should not argue that the LGBTQ+ community is inside the walls of the church. We need to tear down the walls.

## Opening the Doors

We need a fence-destroying spirituality because God destroys the walls that separate people by race, culture, orientation, or religion. We act on behalf of and in solidarity with God and the outsiders kept out by the walls by getting rid of the walls.

Instead of figuring out which people qualify as God's people, let's accept everyone. God's church is for those who know they belong, those who are not sure, people who think they are winners, those who feel defeated, people dealing with the pain of prejudice, and those dealing with their own prejudices. God's church is for garbage collectors, the mentally disabled, the physically challenged, nursing home residents, prisoners, neighbors who do not fit in, and relatives who embarrass us. God's church welcomes all people regardless of sexual orientation, gender identity, or family configuration.

## Setting an Endless Table

When I was at Broadway Baptist Church, we started a tradition of having the Lord's Supper served on Easter by those who had most recently joined the church. I thought it was wonderful to have Communion served by twelve-year-olds and poor people who would not be elected deacons. Some hated it at first and kept hating it.

One Good Friday, a homeless person said, "Pastor, I think my name is going to be in the paper tomorrow. I was arrested for cocaine possession. I don't want to embarrass the church. Someone should take my place to serve Communion."

I said the wrong thing. The minute I said it, I knew it was wrong, but he is my friend, so I asked, "Are you guilty?"

He replied, "It was my girlfriend's, but no one is going to believe me."

I got to say, "Your church does, and even if we didn't, we'd like you to serve Communion."

I know that the point of the Lord's Supper is always that all of us are forgiven, but the table felt bigger that Easter.

## Living with God's Love for All People

Here is what we should do. Stop waiting for others to take the first step and step across the lines ourselves. Speak with kindness and courage when it would be easier to say nothing. Do more than vote right; work for justice and equality.

Work for our congregations to become more accepting. Do more than tolerate our differences—celebrate them. Give up complacency for the way of passionate concern. Be impatient with inequality, impatient with anything less than God's love. Be patient with Universalists who love Jesus.

If anyone is still printing church directories, let me offer a suggestion. Tell Olan Mills that the division of the church into family units is wrong. The most church-like photograph is one great big picture of everyone.

# Chapter 14

# Betting It All On Love

### Rev. Elizabeth Mangham Lott

*Rev. Elizabeth Lott serves as Pastor of St. Charles Ave. Baptist Church, with 25 years in congregational church ministry, and is a writer, activist, and speaker.*

You answer the phone when a member of your pastor search committee calls.

Joe, one such member, called to tell me that he and his wife were leaving my church. "You can do what you think is right," he said, "but we have to worry about our own mortal souls."

He had been part of the committee that originally called me to lead their church and, initially, enthusiastically welcomed my family of four to the congregation. But my sermons were skewing more and more to areas beyond his comfort, and I knew it. We had first reached a crossroads as I preached about the Black Lives Matter protests emerging out of Ferguson, Missouri, in 2014.

Then when Obergefell v. Hodges was positioned before the Supreme Court of the United States in 2015, I began to lay the groundwork for my decision to honor sacred vows exchanged in sacred space for any church member. In other words, I was gonna do gay weddings in the sanctuary. While the overwhelming majority of the congregation was with me, Joe worried for his mortal soul and felt that being associated with me would jeopardize his eternal reward.

"The conversation" about LGBTQ+ inclusion scares a lot of mainline churches because they think folks like Joe will leave. The fear of losing a dozen Joes is what causes congregations to perpetually delay having said conversation. Already feeling the impact of cultural and generational decline in religious affiliation, congregations wonder, "Are we strong enough to talk about this?"

They hope to continue their decades of don't ask, don't tell practices; safe allies are privately identified, and LGBTQ+ Christians play small and quiet in order to keep the peace. To be photographed together in the church directory is one thing, but for a couple to be married in the sanctuary moves the congregation from quietly welcoming to boldly affirming. It's the affirmation that some churchgoers fear.

Will we lose members? Do we have to say it out loud? Can't we just keep the peace and not talk about it? Doesn't everyone already know that our doors are open to all?

After nearly twenty-five years of serving churches, preaching Jesus radicalized me. I was a quiet ally for a long time and thought that was enough. I gradually reached a place where I couldn't stand in front of a congregation in the shadows of Maundy Thursday worship saying, "By this they will know you are my disciples, that you love one another," and then begin to put limits and exceptions on who might receive the fullness of that love. Who can put limits and exceptions on the worthiness of a person to receive and experience the love of God?

That is really what we are talking about when a congregation determines itself to be welcoming but not affirming—you can see, smell, and hear the love, but you can't taste and touch. To me, that sounds a lot like asking LGBTQ+ church members to settle for being three-fifths of a person, experiencing only three of five senses, relegated to distant observation but not full participation in the life of the church and the body of Christ.

To preach Jesus week in and week out required me to consider how wide and long and high and deep the love of God might be. I shared sermons about a man crossing the boundaries of Galilee and Samaria without regard to purity codes, eating with crooked tax collectors and rumored sex workers, restoring those cast out of community because of physical or mental illness, and reserving his harshest critiques for religious insiders who thought they were preserving the right things by keeping "those people" out. "You brood of vipers!" Jesus said, taking on John the Baptizer's words. "How can you speak good things when you are evil? For out of the abundance of the heart the mouth speaks" (Matthew 12:34, NRSV).

"Bless their hearts," my people might say. Those Pharisees meant well. They were seeking God, after all. All that polishing of temple doors and sweeping dust from the steps and making sure people washed the right way and sacrificed the right things. They were earnest. They were just protecting their tradition, right?

That's what we are doing, we tell ourselves. We are just protecting our tradition. All I know is that when the temple tables were only long enough to accommodate the inside crowd, Jesus flipped them over. Then, he had the audacity to go out and make longer tables. (Maybe he really was a carpenter after all.) He found other places with room for everyone who wanted to join him, and those beyond-the-temple places became sacred. Any time two or more people gathered, broke bread, and remembered how he did the same for them, that table was transformed into something of a cosmic kingdom.

So central is this teaching that I began reading it every time we observed Communion: "I give you a new commandment, that you love one another. Just as

I have loved you, you also should love one another" (John 13:34, NRSV). Just like that word of blessing that poured over Jesus at his baptism, "This is my beloved Son, in whom I am well pleased" (Matthew 3:17, KJV)[1], the command to love one another has nothing to do with judgment of worthiness. The command to love comes with no caveats of who deserves love or earns love or ticks enough boxes to experience love. You, dear reader, are worthy of the extravagant love of God simply because you exist; your breath itself is the blessing of God's image placed within you.

So yeah, all that preaching about Jesus means I have gotten to a place where I am going to be as extravagant with love as I can be. At some point I decided that being walked out on or even protested for a welcome being too wide was a badge of honor. After all, Jesus also said, "No one has greater love than this, to lay down one's life for one's friends" (John 15:13, NRSV). However Jesus defined love, it was an active and risky path to walk rather than a lukewarm sentiment muttered at the end of a phone call.

I've hardly laid down my life for my friends, but I have taken a hit or two for them. And it took me a few hits to gain confidence that laying down whatever illusion of a big pulpit pastoring life I quietly thought I was going to have was worth it. Instead, it seems, I'm the pastor who flips tables and builds new ones.

You see, Joe wasn't the only church member to leave over the matter of my extravagant welcome. The one that stung more was a longtime member who said to me over the phone, "You seem to welcome everyone in the world except for conservatives. There's no place for me here." We, too, had disagreed over some of my sermons. But I valued our capacity to disagree and still want the best for one another, to hang on in relationship and community together. That November day, however, I hung up the phone and sat in my office in silence. Then I wept. Truly, I ugly cried. Not because my pride was wounded but because I was sincere in following my call to love. How could I love perfectly if she did not feel welcome, too? How could I balance what she was saying with a call to create holy, radical welcome for everyone who is cast aside, ignored, overlooked, told to stay quiet? Didn't that have to include the very people who don't agree with me?

I carried this with me for weeks, maybe months. In my heart, I kept returning to the Synoptic Gospels' story that we usually merge as the one about the rich, young ruler (Mark 10, Matthew 19, Luke 18). In this story, a man comes to Jesus and initiates a conversation about eternal life. Jesus responds with the central commands of the Jewish faith, and the man already knows them well. So well, in fact, that he's been keeping those commands his entire life. Jesus already knows this man is devout in his faith. In Mark's Gospel he even says to the man, "You know the commandments" (Mark 10:19, NRSV). The young man must have been dumbfounded or looked utterly confused because when he said, "Teacher, I have kept all these since my youth," Mark tells us, "Jesus, looking at him, loved him" (Mark 10:20-21, NRSV). From that heart of compassion, Jesus tells him that the thing he lacks is tied up in his possessions. Sell everything, give it to the poor, and follow me, Jesus says. Release your attachments to what you think gives you value and power and safety. Then come, follow me.

The rich, young ruler is earnest. He is seeking after God. He is committed to the tradition in which he was raised. Of course he is sad as he walks away! He feels like the rules have changed and he's not being acknowledged for his decades of faithfulness. He is shocked, sad, and goes away grieving. And perhaps the most remarkable part to me is that Jesus lets him go. Jesus doesn't equivocate. He doesn't chase after him and say, "Well, maybe you don't have to sell it all. You could bankroll my ministry instead." Jesus is so clear about his own calling and his own mission that he lets the man walk away. He lets him grieve. He allows the man to sit with the shock of what Jesus has said to him.

The story is not really about the money, of course. It's about the man's true attachment to his identity as a wealthy person of the ruling class. The commandments, the temple, the Jewish identity are not the elements truly shaping his heart and mind and spirit to fully honor the image of God within himself and all he encounters. Jesus knows this. Jesus is asking him to give up all of the other stuff that makes him feel culturally comfortable and follow the risky path of the Christ.

I'm clearly not Jesus, but I'm still a really big fan despite the behavior of many of his followers. I love the bumper sticker that says, "This year I want to be more like Jesus: Hang out with sinners, Upset religious people, Choose unpopular friends, Be loving, kind, and merciful, Take naps on boats." I know the pull of what makes me feel culturally comfortable, and it is a siren song. But for pretty much as long as I can remember, I've wanted the path of Christ more, and my encounters with those who questioned my fidelity to our tradition helped me better understand the risks to following that path.

The issue with the longtime parishioner wasn't about my ability or inability to hold space for people with whom I disagree. The issue is really about being willing to release the comfort of what we think our institution and tradition demand in order to follow the heart of Jesus. The safety of tradition and the risk of radical welcome are usually at odds, and I have to choose. I am still actively discerning and choosing.

Nevertheless, her words that day stuck with me and shook my confidence. I decided I needed to be certain that the congregation and I were of one accord. Around that time, Pastor Jim Somerville in Richmond, Virginia, had created a continuum survey to use with his church leadership to gauge where they were in the full inclusion of LGBTQ+ church members. It was a two-question survey with a 1–4 continuum for answers: Where am I personally in this conversation? Where do I think my church should be in this conversation? The brilliance of a continuum is to show that the conversation isn't simply "for" or "against"—so little ever is. On one end was "We condemn homosexuality and exclude gay and lesbian individuals from our membership." And on the other was "We extend to gay and lesbian members the same rights, privileges, and blessings as any other member." In between, the options were to maintain a "don't ask, don't tell '' practice or to welcome everyone except in marriage and ordination.

It was a narrow focus, leaving out swaths of the queer community by name and staying away from the very real matter of gender identity. But it was a start, and I thought it was clever to show the range of where church people might find themselves. I felt a little confidence returning until, within an hour of getting home from church on the Sunday when I distributed the survey, my phone rang.

Deanne was on the other end of the line somewhere between brokenhearted tears and total rage. "How could you put out a survey like this? How could you ask the congregation to vote on whether or not my wife and I should be condemned and excluded from membership!"

I dropped into a chair on my front porch. I had expected pushback from the ones who were afraid I was turning our historic sanctuary into the gay wedding chapel of New Orleans (an actual complaint). In my concern for bringing them alongside and honoring their hesitancy, I completely overlooked how hurtful and abusive that question would sound when falling on LGBTQ+ ears. I apologized to Deanne profusely and assured her I was hedging my bet that our congregation was actually likely to be nearly unanimous in how we responded to that survey. I wanted to demonstrate that not a single person among us wanted to condemn or exclude her. I was right, in fact. It was a costly bet to wager, but the results averaged a 3.8 out of 4 with no 1 or 2 responses.

Still, for Deanne, a queer woman ordained by that same church decades before, even printing the question on those half-sheets of paper made her feel unsafe in a place she had called home for nearly all of her adult life. While the results of the survey brought clarity, and maybe even consensus, the bigger lesson for me was about trusting my own inner wisdom.

I don't know that I regret putting out the survey and allowing it to be a tool that guided us forward as a congregation, but I also know that I no longer feel a need to build consensus around how I express welcome and love. Integrity in leadership meant doing what I sensed deep within me to be right and true even if it was unpopular and cost me popularity. Maybe I decided I was willing to risk my own mortal soul. Maybe I liked the notion of being called a heretic. I just knew I would never, ever again allow someone to question whether or not I wanted them condemned.

Knowing the commandments and the tradition aren't enough, Jesus taught. When a religious leader's fidelity to the temple traditions seemed directly at odds with the Jesus path, he made it clear that they would have to choose whom they would serve. Are you more loyal to the thing or the people? How do you love? How wide and deep and high? Is it revolutionary? Does it put you in or out of favor with the ones who gatekeep religion and call it love? I'm not so interested in religion anymore. I want the revolution.

As for me and my leadership, I decided that following the way that upsets religious people is part of the way of Jesus. Maybe my calling wasn't to maintain the old systems and structures of the church but to awaken to love. Maybe my teaching was to move us from a conversation about weddings and ordination and membership to one about worthiness and belovedness and *Imago Dei*. If welcoming Samaritans and tax collectors and women named and unnamed into Jesus' life made him dangerous, then sign me up for more of that. Even if it means I'm not hireable ever again as a pastor because I flip tables too often and never once remember to polish the temple doors.

It pains me how many stories I now carry of queer people of faith who are struggling to make peace with church, peace with Jesus, peace with the Bible after tremendous spiritual abuse and religious trauma. In my quarter century of church ministry, I know that questions like the one I asked in the survey about condemning and excluding LGBTQ+ are embodied in most evangelical churches. I just didn't always realize that my silent allyship was complicitly supporting harm caused by the church.

Now I realize that our collective hand-wringing about offending Joe and disrupting the peace with "the conversation" has endangered lives. According to the Trevor Project, an organization whose mission is to end suicide among LGBTQ+ young people, "one study of LGBTQ young adults ages 18–24 found that parents' religious beliefs about homosexuality were associated with double the risk of attempting suicide in the past year."[2]

The words preachers teach and preach matter. The lessons churchgoers receive about welcome and love and blessing matter. The messaging about inherent worthiness or unworthiness that LGBTQ+ children and youth and young adults in our pews take into their lived experience matters. I'll never again be part of a church that doesn't fully and unequivocally affirm LGBTQ+ people as every bit worthy and beloved as me, a cisgender, heterosexual, flawed, complicated, truth-telling, middle-aged wife and mother of two. Anything less than that is not love, and I was told that people will know I am one of Jesus' followers because of the kind of love I have for others.

I just don't think we go wrong with opening our hearts to love. A love that is patient and kind. A love that does not envy or boast. A love that is not proud and does not dishonor others. A love that is neither self-seeking nor easily angered. A love that keeps no record of wrongs. A love that does not delight in wrongdoing but rejoices in truth. A love that always protects, trusts, hopes, and perseveres. That kind of love will never fail. I fall short of this kind of love a lot, no question about that. But I am giving myself over, again and again, to the power-threatening, table-flipping, outsider-loving, wine-creating, feast-throwing lover of us all. I'm wagering it all on love, and I have no regrets.

## Notes

[1] Taken from the KING JAMES VERSION (KJV): KING JAMES VERSION, public domain.

[2] J. J. Gibbs and J. Goldbach, "Religious Conflict, Sexual Identity, and Suicidal Behaviors among LGBT Young Adults," *Archives of Suicide Research (official journal of the International Academy for Suicide Research) 19*, no. 4 (2015): 472–488, https://doi.org/10.1080/13811118.2015.1004476

www.ingramcontent.com/pod-product-compliance
Lightning Source LLC
Chambersburg PA
CBHW071007160426
43193CB00012B/1947